The First Date Fix

Copyright © 2022 Trey Richard Hamilton.

All rights reserved. This book or any portion thereof may not be reproduced or used in any manner whatsoever without the express written permission of the publisher except for the use of brief quotations in a book review.

Printed by Amazon., in the United States of America.

First Printing, 2022

Publisher: Patrick and Chenebert

www.thefirstdatefix.com

OBLIGATORY INTRO

0.1 ARE YOU REALLY READY FOR DATING?

1. ONLINE DATING, EVERYONE'S DOING IT.

2. BE PREPARED FOR "THE QUESTION"

3. LOCATION, VENUE AND PLANNING!

4. YOU'RE NOT AS GOOD AT CONVERSATION AS YOU THINK YOU ARE

5. DON'T LET THE HORMONES DO THE PICKING!

6. THIS COULD BE THE ONE, THE LAST FIRST DATE!!!!

7. DRESS UP AND MAKE SURE PEOPLE STARE!

8. BE YOU AND ONLY YOU

9. CHECK IN

10. GET TO THE PASSIONS.

11. YOU DON'T HAVE TO BE ANYWHERE YOU DON'T WANT TO.

12. TRIPPING ON A SIDEWALK DOESN'T MEAN YOU'LL NEVER WALK AGAIN.

13. IT'S ALL IN THE EYES!

14. BODY LANGUAGE

15. DON'T BE THE FACEBOOK/SNAPCHAT/ IG STORY PERSON.

16. THE RISKY CONVERSATIONS…

17. I'LL GET THE CHECK (WHO PAYS!?)

18. DON'T LEAD PEOPLE ON! (REJECTION)

19. SEND THOSE SIGNALS!

20. HAVE A PRE-GAME BEFORE THE DATE!

21. MEET AT THE LOCATION (BE CAREFUL)

22. LEAVE YOUR PHONE IN YOUR DAMN POCKET!

23. MASTER THE ART OF THE FOUR SEASONS

24. THE 3RD DATE RULE

25. THEY'RE NOT MY TYPE!?

26. JUST AS IMPORTANT AS THE ENTRANCE IS THE EXIT

27. DON'T FLAKE!

28. BEWARE THE OVERACTION!

29. ARE YOU A KICKED DOG?!

30. ASK GOOD QUESTIONS!

31. WHO ASKS WHO OUT?

CONCLUSION:

Obligatory Intro

Dating. A practice that's been around for goodness knows how long. The funny thing is, even though it's been around for centuries. The same principles and linear conventionalities remain more or less the same. For real, not much has really changed. Date someone, fall in love, long-term relationship, marriage, or a lifelong partnership. Sounds simple right? The formula hasn't changed that much.

Despite everyone wanting the same thing. The process has become far more convoluted than it ever has been. But, you can get off to the greatest start possible. It all begins with One. First. Date. Personally, I'm a fan of first dates. The excitement of not knowing where it's going to go, who the person really is, and the sheer joy and hope of them possibly being the one. There really is nothing quite like a great first date.

Like anything else, you must have a fun, exciting, and memorable beginning. The first minutes of a sports game, that three-pointer gently grazing the net and that wonderful sound of "swish". The first intro of a movie, the start of a track and field race. The gun BANGS! And they're off, the plane taking off on a runway, that television season premiere, the start of a drag race, the beginning of a book, the start of a classic commercial, and so forth. Did you know 85% of hiring managers know if they're going to hire someone in the first 10 minutes of conversation? 10 minutes! WTF. The first impression always matters.

Always.

You have a limited amount of time on any first date. One hour, maybe two. You should always start out the way you hope to continue.

First dates are important.

Who can forget the opening scene in Indian Jones: Raiders of the Lost Ark? (Dun the dun dahhhhh dun dah duhhhh) Or Bohemian Rhapsody by Queen ("Is this the real life?") What about "Uptown Funk" with Bruno Mars? (Doh, do do dooo do) Or the first episode of Game of Thrones or the first man on the moon? These are things that are etched in your memory. Firsts and beginnings matter and they have a long-lasting effect if done correctly. Every first date you have enables a chance. A chance to make sure you leave with the best possible outcome and spread good vibes throughout the dating universe.

The person who's most sought after will always have an abundance of suitors laying in wait. So you have an opportunity to stand out amongst the conventional and pretty mundane crowd. You're unique, you're different and I want them to see that within you!

That's kinda cool when you really think about it.

First impressions really are everything. In an article by the Psychological Association of Science, they mention that it only takes 3 seconds for someone to size you up in terms of attractiveness and trustworthiness. Granted this is only based on our preconceived historical data based on cognitive biases and filters we've built over the years. But it happens. Which is bloody crazy when you think about it. I found myself thinking why even show up if it's going to be that quick. This is why it's so important to not leave impressions to chance! To dazzle them immediately and make sure you hit the ground in a glorious sprint that leaves them hanging on your every word!

Will they think I'm funny? Like what outfit I have on? What about my job, what if they think it's average? Will they like my shoes? Cute little bangs I spent 80 bucks on? The list goes on.

Dating can be such an energetic and exciting process or it can be something that causes mass and copious amounts of anxiety. Dating can be socially and emotionally draining to a point where you want to say, "the hell with it" and become a frickin' nun. Fear not I can help you get through this! The wonderful and simple truth is, literally anyone can become a fantastic dater and be a delight to anyone they go on a date with. All you need is a willing and positive change of paradigm, the courage to overcome some inevitable fears, and your "WHY". Why have you decided to start dating? What do you really want? Why is it important to you?

As you read this book and put many thoughts and practices here into action. You'll have the skills to go out there and bag that dream partner! If you become good at dating, it's not about being a player, serial dater, or person who's out for the chase. No way! This book is more about refining some skills so you heighten and extend the chances of finding someone you're the most compatible with. It's about giving yourself a fighting chance to succeed or at least get closer to someone you long to be with and know you deserve. It's also about having FUN! If you're genuinely in a position where you're having fun, you really will be a good date. Fun ideas, fun experiences, and memories you create with someone that will last you a lifetime.

I want this for you. I know the joy that came when I connected with someone I still feel incredibly lucky to be with. I want the same for you. I know you can get it.

I truly do. I'm very excited about all of your possibilities and I want you to be excited too! It's not as doom and gloom as some of these atrocious negative dating blogs like to promote. There are good people out there! I promise.

We've all heard the old gurus of dating, there's the corny love doctor's out there and seedy "pick up artists" asking you to go to their seminar and pay $3,000 dollars to learn their shit. Or the Instagram gurus who ask you to pay $2000 dollars just to attend a webinar with this, "One sentence" that will change everything. Well, forget all that nonsense. I'm not a guru. I'm sure as hell, not a self-proclaimed "dating expert". I don't know how anyone could be. Human beings are so nuanced how could one possibly be an expert on what 7 billion people are attracted to?

I've had bad first dates and quite frankly some amazing first dates. You see, about 8 years ago I got out of a pretty bad and loveless marriage (We married young and didn't really end up liking each other too much) I'll tell you one thing. About 7 months after my divorce when I decided to officially throw my hat in the ring and start dating again. I got torn apart. I literally had no idea of how the dating world functioned anymore and I wasn't prepared. I did some stupid things I didn't even know were killing attraction. I was out there looking like a complete moron. Here are some of the silly things I did or didn't do.

- Waited till the 5th date to go in for a first kiss
- Spoke to much
- Sent wayyyyy too many texts and phone calls
- Failed to read the signs
- Didn't pay for the first date all the time
- Couldn't read good body language
- Tried to hard
- Told to much
- Read too much into things
- Dated too many people at the same time
- Jumped into relationships quickly!
- Projected previous pains onto a potential partner
- Selfish as hell

- Over compensated
- Bragged
- Never took anyone seriously
- Kept comparing to my ex
- Drank my own Cool aid
- Partied too hard (Yes there are limits)

I've spent 7years of toiling away in the dating wastelands trying to find out who I am and what I truly want. Like I said before, I'm not a dating guru or a specified psychologist. But I am someone who has been on a considerable amount of first dates because I'm serious about my quest to find my life partner. I've learned so much about dating within that time but I realized before I wrote this book it had to be bigger than me and all my zany experiences. So I'm here to give it to you straight accompanied by some nerdy research I've done.

I met with focus groups of 10-12 people every week at the public library for 3 years. I gathered information firsthand from the people themselves to validate some of my opinions and learn of experiences that invalidated some of my opinions too. I learned brand new ways of thinking I had never even considered before. When I traveled on business trips I would host them at libraries on the weekend via the "Meetup" app so I could get opinions from multiple states. I also coupled the research with some experiences of friends and strangers. I read over 2832 dating articles and 168 books, the more I read the hungrier for knowledge I was. I'm going to make sure you become a master at the first date experience. Not to become an "expert". But to get that person who gets you. To grow old with someone. To have kids or to adventure with them for decades to come. Life is not meant to be alone. It's so much more enriching with someone by your side. You can have it all.

The first impression could be the last opportunity you have to be your best self. The first encounter could be the difference between a soulmate and a shit date. On the first date, there's a decent amount of pressure for both sexes, you're both trying to impress each other with how awesome you are. At the same time, you're not trying to be obvious about selling yourself to a point where you look like a little desperate YouTuber begging for followers and likes. It's a tricky situation if you really want to pick at it. That's why it's important to know who you are, what you have to bring to the table, and most importantly see if you two would be a good match. Fear not though, even the most experienced dater still gets nervous before the big date.

This book acknowledges the nerves, but I want you to have the nerves working for you! To deflect any gradual tension and harness it into a weapon of true self-love and empowerment. When you can always look in the mirror and know, you're not perfect but you're doing everything in your power to be better. To be the person you want to date and to expect what you can give. That's your confidence. That is your truth.

That is you!

You all know some of the basics of dating I would imagine. But I want to take it deeper. I want to give you the ins and outs, a bible of sorts that you can refer to and master so you always make sure the first date isn't left to chance and you know this unconditional and true individual fact...

No matter what happens, no matter how much interest you receive, whether good or bad. You made the best effort you could with what you had. So come what may! Read this book. All the way through and practice some of the chapters. I know if you read this book to the end more than once. You'll get what you deserve and desire. I wish you luck, enjoy this book, and hope you learn something cool.

0.1 Are You Really Ready For Dating?

"To date or not to date that is the question. It's almost as important as Shakespeare's to be or not to be which deals with death".

- **Al Goldstein**

"In order to get over someone, get under someone" That's some of the worst advice I've ever heard. If I can tell you anything first, it's absolutely not to do that, whatsoever. If the body is still warm on your ex, don't worry about it. Relax and take your life into your own hands again till you know deep down you're ready to open up to someone. You owe it to yourself to allow for TLC and life building first, unfortunately, I learned that the hard way and I'm writing this book so you don't have to learn from the pain I've experienced.

I once got out of a pretty toxic relationship with someone. Don't get me wrong now, we both made it toxic. I was impatient, impulsive, made some mistakes and there were a lot of things we could have done better. About two weeks later I bumped into a friend who knew us both. He had let me know that a few hours after we broke up that night, she had sex with another one of my friends. Haha, I know it's kinda crazy right. Hadn't even been 12 hours and she did her thing. Sad thing is, had that not happened we might have been able to fix both of our frailties in the relationship. Now I'm not saying this to "slut-shame" or demonize her. But I'm saying this because actions like that are very unhealthy and all you end up feeling is empty and alone. No matter how much you tell yourself you're tough, it's just sex and you're emotionless.

It's never just sex.

It does hurt and it has damaging effects in the long run.

So ask yourself that question again. Are you really ready to date?

I remember when I got out of a 13-month relationship. After 2 weeks of it being over, I jumped back into the dating world. Let me tell you, I wasn't ready yet again. I was stood-up multiple times and I really didn't know what I was doing. My social EQ with dating was terrible and I had to learn through a lot of trial and error until I figured myself out and dating, for the most part.

I say for the most part because I still lack so many answers. I'm really not an expert. But I've been on more dates than I care to count. I kid you not. I don't say this to brag but I tell you this so you don't have to experience some of my pretty embarrassing stories. So you know I've cut all the bull shit aside and you can learn from my mistakes and geeky research. You see I got tired of making the same stupid decisions and not listening to my gut. Most people need help with dating. I don't give a monkeys how hot you are. Or how hard your abs are. Or how many followers you have on Instagram. You're reading this cause you want some help and I'm excited to take you through this journey.

Never allow society, media, friends, family, anyone, or anything else for that matter, push you into dating. You jump into that world when you're ready, healthy, and excited to look for a compatible mate. Please don't get with someone to make another person jealous or see who's "winning" after the breakup.

It's beneath you and shows a childish-like response you're far better then. Save that s**t for the birds bebe. Ignore the rom coms and the silly reality shows and all that other junk. Go with your heart and gut, always. Trust me, you don't want your bad jaded aura to rub off on someone else who's just trying to get to know you. They have no real idea of the deep and underlying pain you're feeling.

Be patient with yourself and be patient with the process. It will work out in your own time.

Fix yourself internally first, heal your post-dating trauma, when you feel like you're in a better place, go out there and date!

If you're not ready. Give this book a read, fully and wait a few months to apply what you have learned. I want to make sure you're prepared and excited to go out and try the process of dating again!

Before you go anywhere have this internal conversation with yourself:

Why am I dating?

What do I want when I'm in a relationship?

Am I ready to be committed to one person?

Do I want more than dating or even a relationship?

What do I have to offer?

Why would anyone want to date me?

What are my expectations?

Are they realistic?

Does it typically work out with my "type".

Am I ready for real rejection?

When you have a better idea as to what your heart really desires, your actions will easily mirror this and you'll be closer to starting the journey of an amazing, engrossing, and fulfilling healthy relationship.

If you're just a little nervous but really want to be dating, take a deep breath and get it done! It's like most things in life right? We huff and puff about how we don't want to do something because of how uncomfortable it makes us feel, but more often or not once it's done we feel so much better.

I am a fan of dating when done right and I believe in monogamy. But not everyone does and that's okay. If you want to read this for the process of just getting to know someone you're attracted to, so be it. Whatever you need this book to be. Make it so. However don't lead people on and be dishonest with them for your own selfish gains, that makes you a large glowing prick. There's a special place in hell for douchebags like that. **Don't waste someone's time**.

I'm not sure where you're at with dating and what time period you're coming from. But let me start by telling you good and bad. I'll start with the bad first so we can finish this chapter with the good. Because dating is amazing once all the dots connect. No matter where you're at with throwing your hat in the ring and taking on dating by the horns! Dating these days can be vicious and callous and with little to show for your time and effort.

I repeat, dating these days is no joke. It can be brutal, gut-wrenching, heartless, disappointing, cold, emotionless, frustrating, selfish, dishonest and I really could go on but I won't for the sake of not trying to destroy your soul before you've even finished this damn book. The fact is, it's evolved for better and for worse, just like anything else. But it's never a static state.

Technology is growing and getting better at such an astronomical rate it can't help but force and bludgeon dating to grow and adapt too. Platforms such as smartphones, Instagram, TikTok, Clubhouse, Snap chat, and Facebook have managed to extend how people are viewed and contacted. In many cases, they have created amazing relationships. We might have heard that one bloke sliding into someone's DMs and getting married the next year. Maybe even a lady messaging someone they saw on TikTok and now they're in love.

They've also given people the capabilities to destroy relationships too.

You see, "back in the day" dating consisted of meeting someone through friends, maybe your apartment complex, college, coffee shops, concerts, churches, and so forth.

"But wait, don't these things still happen!?"

Hell yeah, they do. But there's a different variable and easier option that's presented itself now. You see 30 - 20 years ago. A man or a woman would speak to that person in the coffee shop, have that meeting in the apartment complex, happily engage with a conversation at church, or even meet their match at college orientation.

That variable now is **ONLINE DATING.**

Those opportunities where people used to meet face to face are diminishing year after year. Because it's far easier and less emotional to connect with someone via the swipe of a finger or the push of a button. You can't avoid technology. In fact, you need technology to advance in life. The ***NYU Dispatch*** attested that "Aiming to stay as far away from [technology] as possible will only hinder someone from advancing themselves in their learning abilities and in society overall" (wp.nyu.edu). So why would you not use technology to date? Why would you get out of your social anxiety-riddled comfort zone and approach someone in a coffee shop, when you could just so easily meet someone and have a conversation on your phone?

It's just easier.

I've had conversations where people have been attracted to someone IRL but hope they match with them on a dating app at some point within their local area. That's 2022's logic. Unfortunately for us, the human mind would always much rather take the easier route. We're very much like a stream of water flowing down the easiest path of least resistance.

We are permanently glued to boxes all around us that slowly influence how we interact with human beings. You wake up, you look at your phone (Box 1), you drive in your car, you look at the screen (Box 2), you go to work and jump on your pc or laptop (Box 3) and you come home and watch TV (Box 4). Or a rotation of box 1, 2 & 3. My point being is that there is little room for real human interaction. Sure you may interact at work, but how real is that? In 2022 we live in a world of rich, instant, and expedient gratification. We want it our way, now, immediately, and at our doorstep. Everything you want for the most part can be delivered to you without even leaving your damn house. That mentality has taken a comfortable warm leather seat in dating. So it's affected how people feel, what they do, how they do it, and who they do it with. The same way someone orders something on Amazon and decides they don't like it is the same way someone can treat your interaction as purely transactional. The same way someone can cancel the uber eats without even talking to a single soul, whilst they're "Prepping your order" is the same way someone can cancel a date without even having a simple audible conversation.

Some examples -

1. If you have a first date planned
    a. They could cancel the day of
    b. They could cancel 15 minutes before or after you're already traveling
    c. They could not show up and you wouldn't even know if they were coming or not
    d. They could have a date 30 minutes after yours
    e. They could be adamant they want to do something different even if you've taken the time to plan something
2. Before your date
    a. Contact with them could just stop on their side
    b. They might forget they even had a date
    c. They could be seeing 5 other people
    d. They could be texting 10 other people
    e. They could find out, where you live, what you do for a living, and mutual friends just by the click of a mouse
    f. You could have a disagreement and you wouldn't even end up meeting
    g. You might find out they've already "matched" with a friend who has a biased experience
    h. They might have already hooked up with 2 or more people you know
    i. They might not like the way you text or speak on the phone

Are you for real!?

Yes, I'm very much for real, for real. Look like I said, with technology people have access to far more romantic partners than they ever have before, so your chances of even getting a first date are not as easy as it once was. The rom-com notion of meeting someone face to face is as antiquated as a corded phone. So even if you made it past the rigorous minefields of actually getting the date. There are still a couple of levels you have to experience before you even actually meet because now everyone has numerous options. And I mean everyone. Even your local UPS delivery guy with the high-rise shorts could be the neighborhood local lothario all behind the magic of a phone screen and you wouldn't know the wiser.

Dating nowadays has so many extra layers to it beforehand, after, and in the middle of the actual date itself. These increasing options create far more obstacles you have to go through because either sex is weighing them out with the abundance of other options they might have.

Yeah sure, you could just show up and know nothing about the current dating scape and you could end up doing pretty well. But I want to make sure you go in all guns blazing. I want to make sure you leave as little to chance as humanly possible. I want your heartbreak to be alleviated. I want you to strike while the iron's hot or escape when the going is good. Ultimately I want you to have the best possible outcome you could have ever hoped for. Hope will get you there, action will take you further and a deep-rooted connection will show you the way.

So I'll ask you again. Are you truly ready to start dating?

Try This Now Part:

Take note of any of the examples before the date or if you have a date planned. How many of them have happened to you? What frequency and what solutions have you tried to make sure they don't happen again?

1. Online Dating, Everyone's Doing It.

"Guys' Number One Fear With Online Dating is the Girl is Chubby. Women's is They're going to Get Murdered." - **Hampton Yout**

Present yourself as yourself!

Men and women don't rush out the door to date liars. So be honest with how you look. Have a recent up-to-date photo. If you get the best angles of your body, that's okay to some degree. But if it's not how you really look, you'll be selling a shoddy product.

Yes, yes! I know you want to present your best self and you sure can, but sucking in your cheeks, sucking in your belly, wearing super baggy clothes to hide how your body looks, will hinder you. People really don't appreciate that stuff. What would you rather? Someone sees you and thinks, "just as gorgeous as the photos" Or "What a liar they're barely recognizable!?" You always want to show photos that show you looking positively radiant and gorgeous, but adding Snapchat filter after filter just isn't realistic. I can't tell you how many women hate it when dudes just post a picture of a topless mirror selfie showing their abs with no face. Or men who can't stand women who post constant Snapchat filtered photos or Facebook angles. It's not real! Do you want a real relationship? A sincere dating experience. Present your real self! It really does seem simple right? But even now people are failing to do that. I hate the truth as much as the next person. But no matter what anyone tries to tell themselves. We're all very visual people and appearances will always matter. Don't shoot the messenger. I didn't make the rules. Blame science.

I have a good idea of what someone might think though. In their minds, they are at least getting their foot in the door for the first date. Much like when a person sends a shitty resume at least hoping to get a screening call so they can sell themselves despite not being remotely qualified. The same applies here, some people just hope that if they show a photo of them 8 years ago when they were in better shape, or perhaps a photo not showing that huge belly they've acquired. Maybe just maybe the other person will enjoy their personality and ride away into the sunset so much that they'll ignore all the things they hid and lied about. I got news for ya, it doesn't work that way. Not even in the slightest. All you get is a person who feels like they were hoodwinked, bamboozled, and led astray. The product that was advertised was indeed, not what was sold. Could you imagine going to see the latest Marvel movie and instead they show some shitty independent movie about a professional chess player who lost two fingers as a child. You'd be pissed! I'm sure the movie of the fingerless chess player is amazing. But not what you paid for.

Note: A big ole belly isn't what the issue is. There are a lot of people who don't care about that stuff and people who are very much attracted to that. But if you lie about that part of you. You're lying to yourself and lying to the person who thinks you're someone you're not. Just be real.

I remember a friend telling a horror story of a first date. The guy showed up and seemed cool at first. After 30 minutes he asked to go to the restroom. 20 minutes went by and she wondered if he was ever coming back from "the restroom". Unfortunately, the man literally ran off! He turned tail and ran! I couldn't believe this story. The sheer shock of it was disgraceful. I asked my friend to show me some of her pictures. They were all "Facebook" angle headshots. She didn't give an accurate representation of how she looked. Worst still the picture was 6 years old, 6 years OLD! That's more than half a frickin' decade. People are not hovering drones. They don't hover right above your head and see you looking up. So stop posting those photos. It will not help your cause.

One single photo or more has an immense power to frame first impressions and design someone's whole personality in their head before they've even met you! These conclusions are false and have an incredibly loose grasp on reality.

Before you turn your nose at the prospect of online dating, remember. Men and women are online dating, more than ever before. Trust me. Just look at some statistics I ran from a Zoosk online dating report for the year 2021. They say that 19% of newlyweds met their spouses online. 19% is pretty significant and this is for marriage. Wow! I thought people were using online dating to ask, "Are you up?" or the obligatory Netflix and chill. Annual revenue in the online dating industry has surpassed $5.5 billion dollars. I had to read that again because I wasn't sure if they were referring to the money spent on porn or something. Half of the single population in the UK/US have never asked someone out, face to face. Holy shit! I read that part of the review and my eyes nearly popped out of my bloody head. That's insane. But it kinda makes sense right? If you meet someone online or maybe even face to face you might not ask them out till you get their number and text them the next day. Man, things sure have changed in the dating world. But trust me that doesn't mean you have to make dramatic changes; it just means you gotta adapt a little and be open to trying new things.

Eharmony had a similar report. 40% of Americans use online dating! 40% I reckon in about 2-3 years it will be 50% maybe even more which means by the year 2025 almost half of or more of the American population will be online dating. I would imagine with the pandemic it's probably going to increase a lot more! Something I didn't think I'd ever hear. But why not? You can literally meet the love of your life by the swipe of a thumb, human beings will naturally take the easiest route they can. Absolutely bonkers! But also very cool. 52% of men use online dating as opposed to 48% of women. That's why you poor women receive a plethora of messages in a single hour. Just ask any single girl who hopped on POF for an hour or so, she'll have stories that will make you cringe and laugh in one fell swoop of emotion. In addition to that, men don't really get hit on at bars, clubs, and the usual haunts if any at all. So it would make sense that there would be more men online. Here's something I actually found really interesting. I'll quote it directly, "For women, online dating statistics show that a woman's desirability online peaks at 21. But, at 26, women have more online pursuers than men whereas, at 48, men have twice as many online pursuers as women". Very fascinating indeed. 53% of people online lie about 3 main things on their online dating profile. Wanna take a guess?

Give it a minute...

Yep, you might have guessed right. They lie about 1. Their Age 2. Their Weight/Height and 3. Their job. I'm not surprised about the last two, these are things that people are so fickle about.

There's a large majority of people out there that turn their noses up at online dating. As if to say because they don't do it, they're inherently in a better social class. But trust me, everyone's doing it or has done it in the past. It's kinda like McDonald's. People like to rag on it and swear they don't go because the food is so trash. Yet they'll always be lines of cars in the drive-through. You know you GO! When someone usually says they don't date online, it comes from one of 3 places. It's either because they were in a committed relationship before the online dating phenomenon, they tried it once and had a terrible experience so they protest to never doing it again. Or they seem to believe that a stronger connection will be maintained if you meet that person IRL.

Rubbish.

They're free to have their own opinion, this much is true. But pay them no mind when you're going through your own experiences and expectations. Remember you're doing this for you and no one else. If it's an easier way for you to meet new people have at it. The right person could be online; you just have to be on there to find them. It doesn't matter what action you take so long as you always take action.

I have more information about this on my Youtube and Instagram. But this book isn't about Online Dating so check some of my stuff out there and we'll move on…

2. Be Prepared For "The Question"

> "To love oneself is the beginning of a lifelong romance." —**Oscar Wilde**

What do you think one of the most obligatory and cliched first dating questions are? Yes, you've guessed it, "So um, why's a great person like you single?". It's the ultimate fishing for answers question. What they're really asking is, "What's the catch? Where's the fine print?". Trust me I get it, in your head you're trying to figure it out. Are they completely absolved from any wrongdoing in their last relationship? Or can they somewhat confess, are there some things they did wrong? The question might never come. But it doesn't hurt to have it subtly in the back of your mind. It's such a dodgy question anyways. It comes across as a slightly passive-aggressive backhanded question, yet people wack away and still proceed to ask it. There's a high risk the wrong person might very well be offended. But there are variations, right? There are more covert ways people have tried and will continue to ask it.

Here are some light examples:

    A.   "What's a gorgeous person like you doing single?"

Offense rating: 3/10 This one isn't too bad. They're actually trying to win you over. They're just a little old-fashioned.

B. "So why are you still single?

Offense Rating 8/10: Still!! Still single!! I'm sorry but did you know me before? Why are you single too, buddy? You can kiss my ass with that nonsense. Are we not two singletons on the same date? Smh.

C. "So what's the catch? You seem too cool to be single"

Offense Rating 3/10: This one is kinda sweet, they clearly mean well, but again. It's a backhanded compliment.

D. "You have so many great things going for you, anything you can't do? Why are you single?"

Offense Rating 2/10: Clearly they're into you. All they're trying to do is make sure you're fallible and you make mistakes just like them, people are far more attracted to someone who makes mistakes and is human. This is called the Pratfall effect. The Pratfall effect in social psychology is the tendency for interpersonal appeal to change after an individual makes a mistake, depending on the individual's perceived competence. Naturally when someone seems too perfect people will always be suspicious. That perfect someone just doesn't exist.

Just tread carefully when you delve into their world. Remember it's a world you know nothing off. Hell, their former spouse may be dead and that's why they're single, now that poor person is going to associate the emotion of death and grieving with you. On the first date no less. Or they could have come out from a physically abusive relationship. I could go on, but you get the gist, sure you can dig but be careful how you go about doing it.

Personally, I'm a little against discussing exes on the first date. But then I also believe that nothing should be off-limits and you shouldn't live with self-imposed rules dating barriers. It's fine to be interested in someone's past in your quest to get to understand them greater, but that shouldn't be your top reason for such questions. It's purely because you're trying to get to know them, not because you're trying to slither around their personal life. But tread carefully and ask questions that have a bit more style and flair to them.

Don't rehearse the answer and don't overthink it beforehand. The fact is you're either single, in a relationship, or married, anything else could just be an excuse for you to have it both ways. Most people are one of the three. There are a million different reasons and no one answer is the same as to why someone is single. When someone asks you, keep it short and simple. Give yourself tiny boundaries as to what you'll divulge if that question comes. No one's putting a gun to your head. Answer what comes naturally and what you're comfortable disclosing.

I want so badly to give you some sentences and retorts you can give as to why you're single. In fact, I actually read 30 articles about this topic (Ya see what I do for you people!). Some of them ranged from, childish, petty, goofy, comedic, and just not real. It fits exactly into the ego-filled narcissistic game-playing madness that dating has become. I'll give you some terrible examples, examples by which you should NOT follow. Just so you can see some of the terrible advice these so-called dating experts have given us.

"Weddings are expensive and I have expensive taste in shoes, vacations, and clothes"

"I don't need a boyfriend to prove I'm worth something"

"I'd rather have a significant income than a significant other"

"I don't need a lady in my life to have fulfillment"

"I'm not single, I'm married to food"

"So far every woman I've met have been unimpressive"

"I'm just lucky I suppose?"

"I just like hanging out in my onesie too much"

"My dog is the only boyfriend/girlfriend I need"

"It's Game of Thrones season"

I swear to god these are all real sentences that people have suggested in some pretty prestigious and long-running newspapers, websites, and publishers. I personally think they're... pathetic. They reek of deflection. Deflection of the pain these people are really feeling. The pain of generally wanting to find someone special and missing the mark or feeling like you were so close and it just wasn't to be. The moment perhaps you realized the whole time they're not who you thought they were. All maybe you were awoken to the reality that people change and not all for the good. Yes, I understand some people are perfectly content to be in single bliss their whole life. But for most of the general population, everyone wants to find someone.

There's not one ounce of realism, truth, honesty, and vulnerability in any of the quotes I grabbed. Yeah sure, some of them are a little tongue-in-cheek and funny. But that's most of the advice out there right now. It's either posted for shits and giggles. Or they come from an angry writer with a lot of pain, axes to grind, and deep-rooted anguish from past relationship atrocities. All they end up doing is projecting that negativity to the world. This ends up being an electronic pandemic of epically myopic views that cling to another person who shares the same pain. I want everyone to embark on this journey with me more so than anything else you've read. The reason being is because I want you to really flesh yourself out when you read this and be honest with yourself.

That's what it took for me to really garner some real relationships and I'm hoping you can find the same too. Look, I know you're thinking, "Get to the meat!! Damn it, I want to know how to master the first date". But I'll keep it real with you. There are a few parts. No. There are a lot of parts where this might be a little "motivational speaker" esque self-reflection. That's what's needed if you want to get it right. But I'm telling you right now if you don't allow any kind of self-reflection things won't change. In order to get better at dating it's going to take honest self-reflection, hard conversations, and the desire to truly change. I believe in you and I think we can change dating together!

I'll never forget when I went out with this one lady. She and I were just vibing incredibly for about 2 hours. It was insane I could have spoken and spoken to her for much longer. I asked her, "what's one of the most important things to you right now, what do you really want?" She looked at me and said...

Her: I want to find love, I've had it before and it was an incredible experience and now I'd like to experience it again.

Me: Wow, I don't think I've ever had anyone be as honest and upfront as you just were.

She chuckled, smiled, and grabbed my hand. Gave me a pretty intense smile and replied.

Her: It's true that's really what I want right now. I'm 29, it's important to me to get as close to that as I can. While I'm still being honest, kids are important to me too. I'd really like to have some in the next 3 years.

My mouth dropped. I was both turned on, excited and very, very impressed with her confidence and clarity of what she wanted. She didn't blow the usual smoke up my ass, she didn't try to play it cool. She was bold, polarizing, and adamant in what she knew was right for her. The vulnerability alone was enough to get me down on one knee and propose right there. Granted, this much forthcoming and external honesty is hard for some people and it's not really their bag. But I'm telling you, try it. Either be raw emotionally or be open to receiving it. The results will blow your mind! You've got to let go of outward stereotypes and pressures of being a little emotionally naked. These days people claim they don't "catch feelings" or don't want to be "thirsty" or try too hard, or even try.

Fuck that shit, go for what you want. I told this story to a female friend of mine. It went like this...

Me: Yeah, she said all that, for real!

Her: Well if I said that to a guy he'd run a mile away

Me: Exactly, cause he's a guy. If he was a "man", maybe he'd think otherwise.

Her: Haha, you're so... corny.

Me: Yeah maybe, but you know it's true!

Her: I just wouldn't want to scare the guy away

Me: Isn't kids what you want though?

Her: Of course.

Me: So if a guy gets shook cause you're honest with him about your intentions is that guy really worth spending time on?

Her: Shit!

Me: I know. I know.

Swear to god this happened at lunch. She and I started laughing about it and I challenged her. Just do it. Tell the guy what you want. Stop wasting your time on boys who are clueless.

After that date me and that lady actually ended up spending about 9 months in a relationship, I loved her a lot. She was an incredible woman. Unfortunately for reasons I can't disclose until the next book, it ended. The fact is, it had me hooked and I knew right then and there I wanted to get to know her and see where this could all go. Look, people, allowing yourself to be emotionally exposed to what you want is very attractive to most people worth their salt. If you truly desire a person of substance and emotional transparency. Be sincere with what you want.

I digress. In general, I came to the conclusion that a response so deep as this should really be down to your own discernment and it has to be YOUR truth. There really is something so vibrant, admirable and, sexy about someone just admitting their romantic verity to a perfect stranger and owning the shit out of it. It allows a deeper sense of connection when you're impactful, polarizing and indubitably raw with your emotions. It expands your cerebral emotional intelligence too. It's one thing to vocalize something to yourself daily. But it's another thing to vocalize your deep amorous desires to a complete stranger, that's true emotional freedom. Anyone who doesn't respect that about you is not the person you're looking for.

Believe that.

Action Time: The next first date you go on tell them the cold honest and vulnerable truth of what you're looking for. If they respond and tell you their raw and vulnerable truth. This is a huge sign. If they respond with something closed off. Or talk around actually giving you an answer, this is slightly bad sign.

3. Location, Venue And Planning!

*"Everyone has a plan until they get punched in the face - **Mike Tyson**"*

It sounds so simple, right? You plan a date, you let them know of the time and the venue and it's a done deal. But so many people fall into silly traps just because they're trying to play it cool or because they're not organized. Man or woman, you gotta have moderate organizational skills to actually start trying to date people.

I can imagine your heavy eye rolls, if you're not punctual you're stubbornly reading this thinking. "Well I'm just late and that's how it is". I say, think about someone else just for a little bit and be organized for them. If you are usually punctual for a first date you're already doing something right. Here are some thoughts on punctuality from the focus group of this chapter.

Benjy: "To be honest I don't really give a shit so long as she's not 15 minutes late I'm good"

Steve: " No way dude, if they're 5 minutes late I walk"

Emma: "Really!? That's harsh. What if they got kids or something"

Kim: "Now we know why yo ass is single"

Steve: "I got stuff to do too. You women need to get off your pedestal"

Chad: "I'm with you bro If they're late by around 10 minutes I go. Unless they tell me they're gonna be late. I mean I'm paying for the date. The least they can do is show up on time"

Emma: "Who said you're paying and planning, women can do that too!"

Chad: "Oh yeah!? When's the last time you paid for a date?"

Emma: "I've done it twice, thank you"

Chad: (Begins to slow clap)

Me: Okay peeps, let's not get personal. Just trying to figure out how you feel about people showing up late for a first date. No jabs. Please.

Katelyn: "So long as they give me a 30-minute heads up they're going to be late. I'm fine with that.

Krista: "a real gentleman shows up on time in opinion".

Brandy: "Yeah I totally agree. Any man who's late just isn't a gentleman"

Steve: "Oh okay, but you ladies can just be late right?"

Sarah: "I'm just happy if the guy actually shows up"

Deshaun: "I mean If I like her, I'd wait for 30 minutes, for real"

Steve: "You're crazy that means they're not interested"

Krista: "Yeah I think it's rude if they're late"

Katelyn: "Maybe something came up, I feel like there's usually a valid reason. Alls I want them to do is show up and plan the date"

Chad: "You know women can plan dates too! It's gotta be said" (Reaches for a high 5)

Steve: "Yeah they're running behind from another date I'm telling you. They gotta go to"

Sarah: "I just bring my Kindle just in case. Being late isn't that bad"

Deshaun: "If you really like the girl and she says she's gonna be late, what's the harm in waiting?"

Chad: "I'm just saying man, don't be late coming from your dick appointment"

Deshaun: "C'mon man"

Kim: "Chad, you a asshole"

Chad: "It's free country, I'm just saying"

Me: "Chad, c'mon man? this is your last warning, please let's keep it civilized"

(Chad gets up and proceeds to storm out. He's never invited to another focus group again)

See, for the most part, people appreciate punctuality and if you're going to be late, just let them know.

Most people hate it when it's the day of the date and they literally have no idea if this damn thing is actually going to come to fruition or not. Let the person start off with a good view of you being organized, excited, and prepared for the date, you haven't even met them yet but you must have the good sense to be a lovely human and prepare for this experience with your time. If you're not willing to do that.

Don't date.

Unless you're dating yourself you always have to take the other person's time into consideration.

Trust me they'll really appreciate it. There are only great things that can be achieved when you plan effectively, I'm telling you. It doesn't even have to be with the planning of the date, you can essentially plan some of the content. Yes, dates should be natural and you should just let it all flow. But it doesn't hurt to have some idea of how you'd like it to go. All you're trying to do is make sure it's a great experience for both parties. I would have at least 3 - 6 topics in mind to really connect and understand the person, maybe even some fun questions too. One thing that I've learned and been told over the years is that planning together builds attraction. You can even toss some ideas at them before the date and have fun editing what you do. However, if you're really into the person who asked you out for the date, be very careful with what you suggest. You don't want them to break the bank on the first date.

Imagine this, you start texting each other after the initial interaction that got you both interested. Then one of you suggests how good the weather's getting. Boom it hits you! You suggest this perfect dessert-only venue that has some cooky designs you've seen on the venue's Instagram page. You send them the link and they're pumped. But here's where it gets super cool. They suggest a venue that has drinks and you guys could tentatively go there if you hit it off after the dessert venue. See that right there! Planning together. I'm excited and I'm not even on this date! A perfect example of when you both work in synergetic harmony.

Or picture this little situation. It's the Halloween season and the person you're very much interested in suggests you guys carve pumpkins together. See how simple that is! Your attraction level heightens because you like how inventive and creative they are with a simple and traditional little plan. Plenty of jokes ensues as you both make fun of how shit both of your pumpkins are. Or one of you creates a pumpkin straight out of a professional pumpkin carvers studio (Trust me I looked it up, there are legit professional pumpkins cutters out there they have, like 45k+ followers). They accidentally flick some seed and pumpkin carcass on their face. You wipe it off their face in close proximity. You're in the kiss zone. Do you pull the trigger and go for it? Or do you save it for later? Who knows! But so many opportunities arise when it comes to originality and planning. The better the plan the higher the chances are for a great first date.

Just make sure you're in "the know" when it comes to things to do in the city or small town you live in. It shouldn't be too hard. You have the internet, the bulletin board in the coffee shop, friends and family to ask what's going on, Facebook (Facebook is great for local events), Reddit, MeetUp, and an abundance of more activities to look into. These will make sure you're ready and locked and loaded to blow them away with a good time. Plus there are always national events going on. Halloween, Xmas season, July 4th, easter stuff, St Paddy's, art festivals, culture days, pride festivals, more festivals, conventions, thanksgiving, strawberry picking, there are always things to do.

Each month marks specific activities and traditions you could have a date to experience them with. Don't worry it's not like you're scouring the internet daily to prepare for dates coming up unbeknownst to you, more so looking for things to do yourself, and if you're lucky enough to grab a date to enjoy it with you. Then so be it! You're just that cool. All of this alleviates perceived dating pressure.

I've heard some bad stories of terrible planning and organization skills. The guy "thought" it was the Johnie's on 5th and not the one on Main Street. Or she thought he meant around 7:00 as opposed to the actual time of 7:00. Or the guy follows up after 5 days of silence to check in about the date, on the day of the actual planned date! By then the ladies made other plans because she thought he was preemptively Ghosting. Or the person who completely forgets! I could go on but you gotta plan these dates. It's not nerdy, it's not eager and it's not being a Clipboard Charlie. It just means you're an adult who cares about people's time. Imagine that "wild" notion, caring about people's time because it's not your own. That's all planning the date really is. Whilst also making sure you've planned it enough so that you both end up enjoying each other's company.

People are shooook these days. They rather say, "Hey do you wanna hang out" Instead of, "I'd love to take you out for a date". It's so simple but we have to be direct and we have to have a plan. Why? If you want to start dating someone consistently and eventually be in a relationship. You have to be clear and direct from the jump. Any essence of ambiguity you allow to fester in the air will only bite you in the bum further down the line.

Spot the difference:

    A.   "So if you want, we can hang out?"

    B.   "I'd love to take you on a date, want to get Gelato this Wednesday?"

    C.   "Let's go out sometime"

    D.   "Yeah we should smoke together and feel the vibes"

    E.   "Let's just chill at my place"

Which one did you prefer? I'm guessing B. Why because it's the one attached with an outcome and a date. I could pick 3 words from that sentence. Date, Gelato, and Wednesday. See how simple that is. I get it, most of us want to "play it cool" and be laid back. Or to be honest, some people really don't care. Think of it this way though. Most people are trying to play it cool. We've come full circle now in society. Where being direct and honest with your intentions is actually seen as polarizing and brave! Always be direct and genuine with your approach. Now

I know, people have lives and aren't always free when you are. But if they say they're busy then this is a good way to gauge their interest. If they respond with:

1. "I can't do Wednesday what about"(Alternative day)

The above is a good sign and is a pretty clear indicator of interest because it's not that day but they'd like to do it another day.

2. "I can't do Wednesday, sorry".

This is a pretty bad response but if you really like them I'd still pursue them. But in my opinion, they're not that interested, so don't hold too much stock in them, I wouldn't really waste my time with someone who can "take or leave" you. But at the same time, you might want to at least go out with this person to see if you guys connect. Their receptiveness might change if you guys really enjoy each other's company so don't pull the parachute just yet. I always maintain that you should push for a face-to-face meeting with just the two of you before you make any real decisions as to what you want. Give this person a chance. But be fairly wary.

As human beings most people don't really enjoy interacting with someone that beats around the bush and can't be honest with their intentions, we're used to it. But it doesn't mean we like it. So you have nothing to lose and everything to gain. A person in my focus group sent me a screenshot of this text.

Him: Yeah maybe we should go out this Thursday

Her: Yeah, maybe

Man, I'm already bored reading that and I'm not even part of that god-awful conversation. See how a lack of direction and planning is. I'd rather have someone say yes or no rather than, maybe. Urgh, the sad thing is these two are in their late 20's. They have no excuse for being poor communicators.

Picture this:

A. "You're going to win the lottery this Wednesday at 3:00 pm!"

Vs

B. "You might win the lottery one day"

One clearly carries more emotional weight than the other.

Be direct and plan (C'mon man!!!)

People are far more intuitive than they ever have been in this age of information and the internet. The old adage of playing hard to get is just that, old. So do yourself a shining favor, just be honest and direct when it comes to making plans. If the person you're dating isn't honest and direct with what they want, they might not be the person for you. When you go on any first date, no one knows anything about anyone. It's filled with so much uncertainty and an opulent sense of mind-numbing ambiguity. Why add to that? Why throw in layers of confusion, "for the chase". Don't be that person. Instead, be a refreshing part of the equation where the person appreciates your lack of game playing and "rule" following. Eventually, they might be so inspired they'll follow suit. So make a solid plan with a date, with a time, and with a nice well lit public venue.

(And no, that's not "your place")

I would go as far as to say, invite them to something you were going to do anyway. That way you're showing a piece of something that you enjoy and is a part of your world. If you both have a good time then you already have a small thing in common and it will heighten the excitement of the experience for both of you. For example:

You: "I'm going to the farmers market to grab some food this Friday, I'd like you to come with me"

Them: "That sounds great"

This safeguards you and puts you in a win, win situation for so many reasons.

1. If they don't show up, you are going to go anyway.

2. It's in a public place and a great time of the day.

3. You get to see them interact with people in the market.

4. The weather will be good.

5. Show them what you like.

We could even get more granular. A new noodle place you want to try out. A store that sells these huuuuuuge cookies that you just gotta try. When you take a date to these locations it's also a great way for you to go out and try fun new things that perhaps you might not have done by yourself. That way even if there are no romantic feelings after the date, you still had a kickass time at that museum you both went to. The two of you will always have that experience observing that awesome new exhibit or being both grossed out by that one dude who was digging for gold in his left nostril.

Above all else, though you have to be flexible and be considerate of the other person's time and availability. I can't stand it when I read all these blogs or Instagram posts that say the most selfish self-centered nonsense I have ever read. Stupid quotes such as, "If they really care for you, they'll work around your schedule", "Real men fit into the women's schedule and realize your busy. If he's worth it he'll stick around". What the hell!? Really?! What about this other person who has their own schedule, too? Dating for some people these days is so woefully one-sided. It's not meant to be a battle of the sexes or us against them. You both have to be equally respectful of someone else's time, within reason of course. I don't want you sending them Google Maps details explaining that you meet at a location that's both 10 miles away and equally 20 minutes travel time. That's a bit much. But try and meet in the middle as much as you can.

No one owes you anything. Let me repeat that for those of you in the back. The sun doesn't shine out your ass. No one owes you anything.

They shouldn't have any hoops they have to jump through to get to know you. You ain't all that. Most people who place an abundance of hoops on someone they don't even know are the same people complaining on social media, "Oh, why can't I find someone special, I'm relationship material". But at the same time, they can be found playing with dating cards where they have a full deck but the other person is left with one or two cards. Dating shouldn't be that geared towards one person. Unless you're dating yourself. Oh, that's not even half of it though.

I read a quote that said this, "I don't want or need anyone, but I'm on a journey of success and I'm very selective of who I choose to take on this journey with me". It's that kind of arrogance that keeps people single and sometimes stops people even trying to meet someone. Most everyone in this world wants someone no matter how much relationship pain they've had in the past. But they swear to everyone they don't really care.

They do, they all do. It's like that one person in the group of friends who swears they're not bothered by being dumped but deep down we all know they are. Everyone wants someone. It's important to be selective, sure I agree, you shouldn't have to need anyone. But everyone wants someone. You shouldn't put yourself on too high of a pedestal. That kind of personality will be very apparent, unfortunately. And for most people, it's kind of a turn-off. Who wants to pursue someone who doesn't want anyone!? Yes, you're a great person I'm sure. But you make mistakes, you aren't blameless in every dating scenario and the person you meet will always be on the same level until proven otherwise, you're the bomb. But you're not THE bomb. At least not yet anyway.

If you're the kind of person who isn't willing to compromise and meet in the middle in terms of availability you're going to be very disappointed, sure you'll get some people who are willing to meet the unrealistic demands of your time. Let's say you do meet someone who is more than willing to bow down to your light brush with dictatorship. They meet you at a location 2 minutes from your house, only when you're free, they pay for everything, plan and prepare for the date and pretty much do what takes to get the first date. Sure the first couple of weeks or months will be fine but eventually, they'll resent you for it and break it off, they'll realize that from day 1 they've been carrying the brunt of the relationship. The first date should enable and build as much reciprocity as possible. If you're one of those people, you're probably reading this knowing it happened to you before. Break the habit! You have to learn to embrace life as it is and sometimes that includes embracing someone else's schedule and planning with it and meeting with them in the middle, any healthy relationship is like this. Compromise and meeting in the middle. Why not start on the best foot possible. Trust me we all get it, we're all busy and have sooo many things going on, fine. But be careful not to "fit someone in". People have a good sense of that and you need to let them know subconsciously you're willing to invest time to get to know them.

You have one shot to make an amazing first impression so do it. If your primary goal is to get something done quickly because you've got a super busy schedule they'll know and they'll feel it within your presence. Plan effectively and give this person your time. Besides if you've done your own research in feeling this person out, you probably already have a good idea that time spent with them will be more than worth it.

Above all else keep it short and to the point and you want to leave the date on the highest note possible. You do that so there is excitement for the next date and both parties leave with happy thoughts of what's next to come. If your date goes too long, the other person may run out of energy and be done after 90 minutes. So be careful of their time and just enjoy the moment.

Take it from me and anyone else who has had an amazing or terrible first date! It really does greatly affect where it's ultimately going to go. I know it sounds pressure-induced and nerve-racking but your romantic future, should you choose to accept it, can be defined by an incredible first date. Is there a magic first date place? In short.

No.

The general consensus is people want to be around someone who has a sense of certainty in what they do and the choices they make. So when it comes to suggesting a date be original and don't ask them what they want to do or if you hope they enjoy the place you're taking them, just go with it. If you take them to a place that you really enjoy and they don't really like it they may not be the person for you. Don't get me wrong you don't have to enjoy all the same things, but it helps. Or you may have just chosen a poor date idea. Try to be sure and concrete with what you prepare. If they don't like the date you've planned and paid for and you're still into them. Give them a cheeky smile and suggest they plan the next date.

There's nothing worse than someone who hates an idea or a plan but can't suggest anything better. Don't worry though, all is not lost. If they really think you did a terrible job on planning, make up for it with awesome conversation witty banter, and a smile that just won't quit. Again, that's only if you really like them, cause to be honest if they care more about where you've taken them rather than you just being there. This is not a person you should be dedicating too much of your time to, repeat they are not keepers. Usually, the place you take someone is just a filler to create an environment where you two could possibly mesh, anywhere.

They'll never be a perfect venue. Dating has never been a one size fits all shoe. So let's start very simple and break it down. You must first mentally assess where you met this person. For example, if you met them in a bar. Do not allow that to be your first date, going to a BAR!. So Where did you meet them? Online? Apps? Friends, Grocery store? Gas station? Police station? Dinner party? Sacrificial Ritual? Wedding? Shopping Mall? Professional Mixer? Either way, depending on where you meet them it will really set a clear stage with where you want to start getting to know them.

Above all else take this into consideration. The first date is merely to determine if you may or may not have even a flicker of romance and connectivity, then you water the grass from there.

A. "I met them on a dating app"

Meet them in public and accept nothing else. Meeting someone for a first date at their house is one of three things and I really can't paint it for you any clearer than I am right now.

1. They want to have sex with you.

2. They would like to wear your face on their next killing spree.

3. They are completely clueless about the general concern for the safety of the other person.

Either one is terrible. Especially the face wearing. Trust me I've been on dates with someone who was boring as hell and super annoying and it was great cause I could just end the date and go on my merry way. I didn't have to worry about being trapped at someone's birthday party or sitting watching a basketball game with someone for all 4 quarters! Or worse have a 2-hour dinner and have such a mind-numbing devastatingly painful conversation. Just be careful and make wise decisions. You just have to be a little on your toes and be careful when it comes to dating online. You just never really know or have a good idea of who the person is till you meet them. But we'll get more into that later

B. <u>Met them at Chris's divorce party</u>

Ha ha, ignore the title. But if you met them in real life. That's a win-win. In my humble opinion, I much prefer an old fashion face to face introduction. At this party, you two might have had a discussion about something you enjoy doing. Maybe you spoke about always wanting to try that new Taco place on 5th. Or the new space exhibition at the museum. Or how much you both love walking your dogs at the state park. Do something like that! I'm assuming if you met them IRL. There was something you connected with. Both artists? Take them to a paint night, as you both laugh at the amateurs presenting there. This also means that when you meet someone you can make sure you're generally trying to get to know them so you can experience mutual passions on the first date. Man, how awesome is that! When you meet someone face to face you don't have to play it safe! You can roll the dice and do something you both might love!

KISS (Keep it simple stupid) Don't be a cliche. Please don't go out of your way to do something that is a 4-hour experience on a 1st date. Dinner will take 60 minutes or more including the travel time to and from the dinner place to the movies we're talking 90 minutes for the movie. It's a 4-hour experience.

A simple round of drinks, coffee, or even a walk should suffice. So keep it short and to the point, enough to warrant if this person is worth more of your time. Or you can do what every other person does and bore them in the movies, then they'll be planning their escape route, I can guarantee you that.

Short and sweet and keep it neat. I get it, maybe you're jaded or maybe you're over the whole dating thing so your mind is numb to all the dates you planned, prepared, and showed up to. All to have nothing happen and the person not remotely interested in you. But make an effort to keep it light, fun, and interactive. I know for a fact your date will very much appreciate it. Enjoy getting to know each other and couple that with a great activity or an area that promotes full and genuine conversation. You don't ever want to go on a date that's so boring and feels like you're signing an offer to a house. Have you ever purchased a house? On the final signing day, you have a borderline book worth of papers to sign and someone reading over all the laws and regulations. It's incredibly tedious. Don't let a person ever feel that way about you. At least with a new house, you have the possibility of getting equity. The same can't be applied to a shitty poorly planned first date.

Please, please go outside of your usual first date idea and do something just a little bit original, just a little. I'm not asking you to break the bank or schedule fireworks. But make even the smallest effort to what you might usually do. You have a grand opportunity to allow them to see a side of you that maybe you don't always display. So, show them and get a little vulnerable with your planning. It doesn't always have to be this way but get imaginative.

Everyone seems to know the perfect place to meet someone for a first date. But to be quite honest the opinion is so subjective it varies. There are some people who swear by dinner but I'm a bit wary of that, especially from a male perspective. Let's say you have 4 first dates in a month that were all dinner and each meal came to around $60.00. That's $240.00 a month on dates. That's $2,880 a year! On first dates. That's a lot of money. So you have to take small pieces of information like that into consideration.

Like I previously mentioned, drinks or short coffee dates are always a winner in my opinion. It's not too romantic or pressure-inducing. The beauty of drinks or coffee though is it allows flexibility. If there's no chemistry and you both don't get along. You could cut your losses after 45 minutes and go about your day/evening. If you absolutely both get going like a house on fire, it could be the rest of the night. You go home thinking, "holy shit what an amazing date! I can't wait to see them again". I think for the most part you have to go to a place that maximizes conversation, makes you both comfortable, and has a lot of space so you don't feel so confined.

Believe me. I know these dates to a coffee shop or drinks aren't lavish but, think of it this way -

It's about 7:30 in the evening. She's running a little late but shows up at Belle (Wine Bar) at around 7:40. You greet her and share a hug, she sits down and you two engage in a little conversation about her journey there as she apologizes profusely for being late. You think it's so sweet that she would be so considerate as to apologize for a mere 10 minutes. You like that already! Drinks are ordered and a conversation ensues about your favorite Schitt's Creek episode and how much you both love season 2. Then you both get into a flirtatiously heated discussion about who's the best character. After a few laughs the topic of comedies comes up and you both start laughing about the show Friends.

You both adore Phoebe. Things start to heat up a bit as you compliment her shoes and she says she likes your smile. You start talking about dating and how different it is from when your parents did it. Maybe you even share funny dating horror stories. The conversation deepens and you start talking a little about projects you're working on, goals, hopes, and dreams. She shows you a photo of her dog, you show her a photo of your cat. Then you both start gushing about the love of animals you both have. An abundance of other discussions ensue. But wait, it's 10:20?! Crap where on earth did the time go. You walk her to the car, on the way you notice a piece of cotton has been trapped in her bangs, you get in close to take it off. The kiss zone is right there. Do you go for it, what happens next...

This is all from a mere 2 drinks. I'm telling you right now, whilst the venue is important of course, the conversation is just as important so having a great venue is merely icing on a cake. No one ever complains about the stadium when their favorite team is playing or how awesome the field is. Of course not, they just care about the game being played there. So should you.

We still have dating gender norms in place so typically a man would ask and plan the same date. I've rarely heard of a great many scenarios where the woman plans and asks the man out on the *first date*. It happens and I think it's great and progressive when it's done but it's definitely a rarity. So when you're planning this, be sure to take the other person's interests, personality, hobbies, and geographical location into your planning process. After all, you wouldn't want to take your date to a Vegan festival not knowing he has a super meat-based diet. To be honest that would make for a pretty funny story.

When you're thinking about the venue of the date you always want a bit of activity and downtime. Even if it's something simple, like eating cookies together. You can still walk down a nice romantic street eating ice cream. Or walk along the pier while eating a hotdog and take in the late summer breeze just before sundown as the waves of the ocean gently clap against each other in the distance. Or you could walk down a nice romantic beach and just talk about the ocean. Conversation + Activity is always a good look too. When you have something that ticks all those boxes it alleviates both parties' concerns about having long-drawn-out conversations that are just, plain boring. At the very least you both have a fun minor activity. There's also a matter of temperature.

A study was conducted with a few people at Yale University. Your attraction and judgment of a person's character can be influenced by something as simple as the warmth of the drink that you may hold in your hand. In the October 24, 2008 issue of the Journal Science, Yale University psychologists demonstrated that people judged others to be more generous and caring if they held a warm cup of coffee and much less so if they had held an iced coffee. So what does this mean? Have your date in a warm place. Physical temperature adds to how we see others, it affects our own behavior on a date, too.

It really is as simple as physical warmth allowing you to see your date as a warmer person, it can also cause you to carry a warmer personality. Weird right? But I tried it and it definitely added an extra element to the date. But it doesn't stop there, the power of temperature on character assessment has been supported by recent brain imaging studies, too. For example, the experience of a hot or cold stimulus has been shown to trigger strong activity in the insular cortex.

Absolutely wild! Science has such a large part to play when it comes to attraction. All you have to do is harness it and bring it into every dating equation so you can give more space to a possible romantic conclusion.

But remember even if it is still a simple coffee (In a warm location) you can still add an activity, for example, if you feel like you're both pretty comfortable after an hour or so you can throw caution to the wind and have a stroll down the street and hold hands as you do so. Trust me, there is always room for romance.

If you wish to stay inside I would suggest a fairly large place with high ceilings. A bad location would be a tiny little cafe where everyone can hear about your intimate details and laugh at the potential awkwardness of your first date, not the worst thing in the world but it's a no for me.

4. You're Not As Good At Conversation As You Think You Are

Be brave enough to start a conversation that matters.
- **Margaret Wheatley**

Yeah I know it sounds harsh but you're not.

For some strange reason, humans have a natural tendency to want to parade themselves around and only talk about what we like and find interesting. I remember I left one date thinking I had it in the bag and she was way interested.

I didn't.

I did not, indeed, "Have it in - the - bag".

I think I spent an outrageous amount of time talking about myself. Don't get me wrong I'm not saying in order to be a conversationalist you have to not talk about yourself at all. But you must strike the perfect balance. You gotta listen and study books on communication. I'm not kidding. After realizing I had turned into a borderline narcissist on that date I bought, 5 books!

- How to Win Friends and Influence People

- The Charisma Myth
- The science of likeability
- Be THE communicator
- How To Talk To Anyone

The books helped me to not be so selfish in communication and really take the time to listen and get to know someone. When I finished all these books it really changed my dating experience, all because I learned how to communicate better. I would practice all these new skills because I wanted to be a better option for anyone who wanted to find love as much as I did. I really wanted this to affect all aspects of my life. Not just dating. You can't develop or feel a connection if you don't feel like they're listening or really get you. If you can't adequately conversate on what you bring to the table as a person your chances of success are slim to none. So pull up a chair, don't interrupt, let the person talk, and be the master communicator!

In 1874 Benjamin Disraeli and William Gladstone both rallied and competed to obtain the position of prime minister for the United Kingdom. On one rare occasion, both men had the pleasure of dining with a lady by the name of Jennie Jerome, Winston Churchill's mother. Here's what she said about conversing with the two of them, separately:

"When I left the dining room after sitting next to Gladstone, I thought he was the cleverest man in England. But when I sat next to Disraeli, I left feeling that I was the cleverest woman."

So who won the election?

Disraeli.

Why? Because he took the time and skills needed to master the art of conversation. The art of conversation will always be about making the other person feel important.

Disraeli spent the whole evening asking her inquisitive, sincere questions and listening intently to her responses. He genuinely wanted to know everything about her, and he steered the conversation toward her. She sang like a canary and was more than willing to share some wisdom. No matter what anyone tells you, people love talking about themselves.

You need to do what you can to really listen, you can do it. It's crazy how listening to everything makes you a super communicator. But don't be scared. If you can't help yourself and have to interrupt, only allow it to be so, when you strongly agree. Don't interrupt with a sentence, instead interrupt and say, "me too!". Who would possibly be upset about interrupting when it's to agree with a point and see that you're both kindred spirits. The more open you are to the person scintillatingly so, the better the conversation will go. Last time I checked, relationships do not move along by exchanging grunts and rugged glances, leave that shit for the Twilight movies.

> "During a conversation, listening is as powerful as loving."
>
> — Amit Kalantri, **Wealth of Words**

Being a great communicator just builds such a good foundation of enriching mutual likes and sometimes fun dislikes to build upon. A burgeoning and passionate sexual attraction can always be built just by enjoying the beauty of a synergetic conversation that arouses emotions and feelings of potential and future bliss. Have sex with each other's minds before you even get close to ripping each other's clothes off!

I'm serious. I've only ever been in love 3 times and they all started with us having some pretty amazing conversations. I remember leaving each one of those first dates with such an extra pep in my step. You'll rarely hear anyone come back from a date and say, "Oh goodness, they're just so good at having a wonderful conversation. It'll never work". See what

I'm saying!? It's such a great skill to learn because it stretches much further than dating. If learned continuously it can affect your whole life and every interaction you have will be all the sweeter. Try it! Really take the time, maybe one 30 minutes a day. 30 minutes of communication skills study and watch your life flourish in ways you never quite imagined possible. Or if 30 minutes is too long. Just watch a 10-15 minute video on YouTube. This is the age of free information. You can do it!

This will all get better the more you take it seriously and work on becoming a good conversationalist. "But how do I become more interesting?". I'll tell you…

First off, hold out for as long as you can before you talk about your job.

It's not a bad thing to do so, but everyone talks about their job and it's just so cliched at this point I don't know why you wouldn't at least try to think bigger. But society once again has reared its ugly head. So social circumstances of small talk dictate you have to bring it up. I say, don't bring it up till they do. Nobody wants to hear, yeah I work at Nordstrom's and watch Netflix every day when I get back from work. Not a bad thing, but have some diversity with what you do. If that's literally all you do. Change it up a bit.

You are far more than binge-watching TV, there's gotta be something you really love. Share that! If that truly is all you do on a weekday basis. Do new things! Get social, find a hobby. Start doing things that scare the shit out of you. Trust me it's like anything else when you go through the refiner's fire. It might be a bit daunting and intimidating at first but once you get used to it, you'll love every moment. Then you'll be filled with small facets of great conversation because you truly live a great life! Not just for the purpose of dating anymore. But I promise you, it will become a part of who you are. Have a deep lust for life, it will help you find your person!

When having a conversation with your date, pay special attention to the words that someone uses too. Loud and rapid speed is good indicator that someone is pretty interested. Especially if they're using words such as —like "absolutely" and "definitely"—and their sentences are filled with pretty inclusive words like "we," "with," and "Us".

For example :

    A. "So where are you taking us tonight."
    B. "That sounds just like us"
    C. "We should totally do that one day!"
    D. "Oh I definitely agree"

Dead giveaway. Dead giveaway! This person is more likely to be interested. But then there's the flip side and their carefully crafted responses such as, "Maybe," "I guess," "sure," and my personal favorite, "Perhaps". This person is still on the fence about you and is in the mutual zone. Don't worry about that too much. If the date comes to an end and they're still mutual. All hope is not lost. There's still an opportunity. They just might not be interested as quickly as you are. I'm sure you're a catch, but when it comes to attraction remember everyone has a different pace. I always say give someone at least two to three dates to really figure that person out and get a good bearing on where you stand in their eyes and of course how you feel about them. You just never really know. For example with my partner and I, she was very shy initially and I knew she was interested to some degree. But I didn't know at what length. So be patient.

If you aren't good at having conversations on a first date here are some things you really shouldn't say if you want to build any kind of attraction:

    A.   "I'm so nervous right now"

It's not the worst in the world, but it's an abused sentence. What you might have done is nullified and killed any immediate attraction. You have unknowingly submitted your application to the friend zone and you better do whatever you can to make sure you can build attraction and at least connect with them after such a needy statement. Being nervous is natural. But they don't need to know. At least not yet. Imagine this, you're a CEO for a Fortune 500 company, and someone interviews for a VP of a sales job. They come in, sit down, shake your hand and say, "I'm so nervous right now".

What's the first thought that comes to your mind?

Exactly!

This is not the person you know is going to kick ass and take your sales team to the next level. This is not the person who is going to smash through financial ceilings and give the company revenue you can only dream of. First impressions mean everything and a simple utterance such as that can change the attraction landscape. Now you're sitting there thinking, "A first date isn't a job interview". Oh no? It's exactly like an interview. Not directly of course. But when you're on a date you ask questions to essentially see if the person is up for the task to be your potential "boyfriend/girlfriend/person". So sometimes the mentality might very well be the same.

Telling someone the first time you meet them that you're "nervous" will not make them fall head over heels for you. But what it might do is allow them to shed a small ounce of pity for your predicament, much like a lonely little cat purring outside your door for milk, "awww it's shy". Do you want pity or someone to feel bad for you? I'm putting all my savings in this bet and guaranteeing you they will not fall head over heels for your nervous disposition. It may or may not come across as endearing, but you want a strong first impression. Forget what the movies have taught you in these rom-coms or shitty episodes of The Bachelor and just keep that little piece of information to yourself at least for now.

B. "Wow, you look hot!"

A statement like that could be said to anyone walking down the street who looks moderately attractive. God, it's so overused undercooked, and just *sigh* not that good. Everyone looks good to some degree, right? How do you think that statement works with someone who's very attractive? It holds far more weight when you actually know the person. But you don't know them yet. Imagine if you have a red shirt that you wear one day at work, people tell you, that's a redshirt. You walk down the street and someone says, "That's a pretty red shirt". You head to the gym and someone says, "that's a red shirt, buddy". I could go on. Sounds weird right? Thank you Captain Obvious. But that's exactly how very attractive people feel after a while. Sure it sounds nice at work or maybe even from strangers occasionally. But when you're on a date with someone you might potentially want to be in a relationship with and they hear the exact same line they've heard from everyone. You are thrown in the same bracket as colleagues, strangers, and generic people. Yikes.

So be careful and sparing with that comment. Instead, comment on the time they've clearly spent on their outfit, that's a unique style only they have right? If you're going through compliments, throw them out over things that take time and a genuine effort has been consciously made for you! For example, "I love your hairstyle. Did you get that done recently?" perhaps "That's an awesome shirt most guys can't pull off purple but it's working on you". Sounds like a little bit of an effort. But what's wrong with making a concentrated verbal effort with someone you're trying to get to know? When you're present and engaged it shouldn't take too much mental capacity to give them an unconventional compliment. Remember you're different. You're THAT person.

C. "I want to know as much about you as I can"

Look, this is sweet. I get it, you're enthralled by how awesome they are. You're craving to get to know them and how you might win them over. But for the person on the other side. It's so vague that they don't really know where to start, you'll be sitting there with an awkward silence as they try and scramble together a sentence and a brief elevator pitch as to who they are. Trust me you don't want to know ALL about them. I did this so many times at the beginning of my dating experiences, it's not really the most effective. Let it flow naturally. Of course, you want to let them meet the real you but don't put all your cards on the table. Just a small slice of mystery is all that's needed, just chill with the information digging, ask one question and expand on that politely.

Remember to get to the "WHY". You want to know all about them. Sure, but not all on the first date. Imagine if you watched all 4 of the Avenger's movies crammed into 1 hour. How would you feel? Ever binge-watched an entire season on Netflix in 4 days or even a weekend? When you look back a few days later, it's actually really hard to recollect all the key plot points. In order to adequately assess if this person is for you. Pace everything out.

Luckily I did some research so you don't have to. I stumbled upon a pretty impressive 15-page study by renowned psychologist Arthur Aron and some supporting psychologists who assisted him in the study. It basically illustrates that a deep affection can be easily created by either of the two strangers asking each other a series of questions which his studies derived to be **critical in building an intimate connection**.

How many questions? Just 36.

Yep, essentially if you ask these 36 questions and master them. I tried them, they actually work, in the sense that I did feel a pretty close connection just on the first date. It's a pretty cool study, the higher you get from 1-36 the deeper and more meaningful the questions get. The general thought process behind the results of the study is that a unified openness and unguarded conversation builds intimacy. Doing this on a date, the first date no less is intense and requires a high degree of bravery and the right kind of personality to accompany you in this adventure.

Want to know what the 36 special questions are? ;)

1. Given the choice of anyone in the world, whom would you want as a dinner guest?

2. Would you like to be famous? In what way?

3. Before making a telephone call, do you ever rehearse what you are going to say? Why?

4. What would constitute a "perfect" day for you?

5. When did you last sing to yourself? To someone else?

6. If you were able to live to the age of 90 and retain either the mind or body of a 30-year-old for the last 60 years of your life, which would you want?

7. Do you have a secret hunch about how you will die?

8. Name three things you and your partner appear to have in common.

9. For what in your life do you feel most grateful?

10. If you could change anything about the way you were raised, what would it be?
11. Take four minutes and tell your partner your life story in as much detail as possible.

12. If you could wake up tomorrow having gained any one quality or ability, what would it be?

13. If a crystal ball could tell you the truth about yourself, your life, the future, or anything else, what would you want to know?

14. Is there something that you've dreamed of doing for a long time? Why haven't you done it?

15. What is the greatest accomplishment of your life?

16. What do you value most in a friendship?

17. What is your most treasured memory?

18. What is your most terrible memory?

19. If you knew that in one year you would die suddenly, would you change anything about the way you are now living? Why?

20. What does friendship mean to you?

21. What roles do love and affection play in your life?

22. Alternate sharing something you consider a positive characteristic of your partner. Share a total of five items.

23. How close and warm is your family? Do you feel your childhood was happier than most other people's?

24. How do you feel about your relationship with your mother?

25. Make three true "we" statements each. For instance, "We are both in this room feeling ... "

26. Complete this sentence: "I wish I had someone with whom I could share ... "

27. If you were going to become a close friend with your partner, please share what would be important for him or her to know.

28. Tell your partner what you like about them; be very honest this time, saying things that you might not say to someone you've just met.

29. Share with your partner an embarrassing moment in your life.

30. When did you last cry in front of another person? By yourself?

31. Tell your partner something that you like about them already.

32. What, if anything, is too serious to be joked about?

33. If you were to die this evening with no opportunity to communicate with anyone, what would you most regret not having told someone? Why haven't you told them yet?

34. Your house, containing everything you own, catches fire. After saving your loved ones and pets, you have time to safely make a final dash to save any one item. What would it be? Why?

35. Of all the people in your family, whose death would you find most disturbing? Why?

36. Share a personal problem and ask your partner's advice on how he or she might handle it. Also, ask your partner to reflect back to you on how you seem to be feeling about the problem you have chosen.

Once the final question is answered by both parties then what? The study calls for both of you to stare into each other's eyes for 2 - 4 minutes. I'm an extrovert and even for me, it was excruciating at first. But we were both very glad we did it. After the awkwardness vanished we wanted to try for four minutes. It was a very enriching experience. We dated for a year after that. So essentially my rate with that test is 100%.

Just remember that any kind of interaction when it comes to

dating should be "**non-outcome dependent**". What I mean by that is you don't speak to them or go from sentence to sentence with an end goal or specific outcome. But you ask questions, make statements in order to get lost in the potential of an enriching connection.

5. Don't Let The Hormones Do The Picking!

> "We never regret the love we give,
> We regret giving it to the wrong people ..."
> — **Samiha Totanji**

One of my favorite guilty pleasures is Millionaire matchmaker. If you're a fan like me you'll notice one of her favorite phrases is, "The penis does the picking" she means that most people are very attracted to physical attributes first (Moreso men). That's okay, for the most part, that's just how we're biologically wired. But please, please whatever you do, do not let that be the anchor of your decision. Looks fade and if someone isn't the sharpest tool in the shed, they'll probably be that way for far longer than they look good (Just sayin'). It's the classic line of "Looks fade, but stupid is forever".

Just because she's extremely good-looking or he's so handsome! It doesn't mean the two of you are compatible. If they're incredible in bed on the first date, please do not use this as an indicator of relationship compatibility. The sad thing is everyone has been guilty of making that mistake before and that's okay. When you're in toxic dating scenarios, it's important to look back at them as a learning experience. Not doomed to make the same mistake again and again. Be careful not to fall into such an easy and predictable trap, bad habits are very hard to get out of, especially when it comes to who you date.

For example, one of my favorite personality traits is someone who demonstrates a high degree of reciprocity. Meaning if I ask her how her day was, it's nice when she answers and then asks me how mine was too. It's very simple, right? But I can't tell you how many people I've dated and something as simple as asking how my day was, just isn't present. My point is that you must have a higher sense of actual wants besides a banging body and an ass so big you can see it from the front. So chill out and don't get swept into the hurricane of your bodily hormones spiraling out of control in that head of yours. Learn from your mistakes and begin the groundwork of expanding reasons why you're into someone. If someone's hot, they're hot. That's great! But you have to make sure the scales are diverse when you look at the assortment of personality traits and general contributions they might bring to any kind of relationship.

I would actually recommend writing something down on a google doc, a piece of paper, or your notes section on your phone. Put it into 3 categories.

1. "Not interested at all" (RED)

2. "Mutual" (Orange)

3. "I'm very much interested" (Green)

I'd do something like this:

1. **Red:** Bad manners, impolite, uneducated, no passions, rude, lack of ambition, too quiet, poor conversationalist, stinky, extreme political views

2. **Orange:** Political affiliation, financial background, family upbringing, 5-year plan, friendship circle, hobbies, religious yes/no?

3. **Green:** Attractive, intelligent, motivated, spiritual, empathetic, kind and benevolent, funny and charismatic

Now of course this is just a brief example that I've come up with, but if you are sincere about dating and want to make sure you truly find a deeper connection. It's nice to narrow down the herd a little. You see, someone could be a green and that's a BINGO! I'm into them. Someone could be an orange, they're attractive but you want another date to see and get to know them more. If you come up with something like this ahead of time you'll be able to make better decisions before and after the date and won't be mesmerized by how smoking hot they are. So write them down and figure out exactly what you want if you haven't already.

Remember to be very careful when selecting wants vs needs. Decide what is negotiable and what you absolutely refuse to put up with. When I say negotiable I don't mean for you to sit down with your date and get a checklist out. Sitting there with them asking them what personality traits they're willing to get rid of. But I mean, things you'd be okay living with. For example, I hate country music, but I could still fall madly in love with someone regardless of musical taste. Or something like, I can't stand camping. But if I was in a committed relationship it would be no skin off my nose to do it for the woman I love. So you see where I'm going with this, just think about the things you could deal with and the things you absolutely would not! Because no matter how perfect someone may seem there are going to be some things you just don't agree on or even like.

Following this process will save you so much time when you're out there looking for a potential mate.

What's important though above all else is that you don't become a slave to your bodily desires and go for the girl with the biggest boobs or the guy with the huge pecs and massive arms. Sure if you haven't experienced being that impulsive with looks then have at it! If you truly want to experience the quick and very instant self-gratification of following only your hormonal passions, you can. But be very wary, instant gratification can yield long-term damaging effects. You'll end up having too many of those sexual experiences and could be slightly out of touch with what dating reality really is. I'm trying to help you find something meaningful. But realistically, we all know how the story goes. We know how it ends, physical attraction has a short shelf life and will eventually rot away at you and your relationship if it's the sole determining factor for you two being together. So whilst it's okay to think, "Wow they're so SEXY!" This shouldn't be the only real reason your interest level is high. It should really only be an addition to the already wonderful things this person has going for them.

I kind of look at a physical attraction like some of the best set pieces in the movie. You know, the action scenes. You have a fight with the penultimate villain, the car chase, the motorcycle making it across the bridge and a huge explosion as our hero walks away, victorious. All those things in action adventures are great. However if your movie lacks a great plot and very deep character development arc, you're left with something along the lines of Batman Forever or some shitty Transformers movie.

What you want is a great action and set-piece coupled with a great storyline and drawn-out submersible character development. That's the start of a very cool dating scenario.

So if you can. Hold of sex just for a little bit. I want your world to be rocked in the bedroom. But I also want you to exercise a slight bit of judicial wisdom.

TREY HAMILTON

6. This Could Be The One, The Last First Date!!!!

*Assumptions are the termites of relationships. — **Henry Winkler***

In some ways, you're halfway there.

Why? Well if you've asked someone to join you on a date. They're probably neutral, which means it can really go either way. Better still there's a strong chance they could be very interested. Now on the other hand, if someone's asked YOU out on a date, they're most definitely interested. I've never known anyone to take the time, put themselves out there, and ask someone out on a date for shits and giggles. It usually comes with intention. Fortunately, you decipher what the intention is and if it fits in with what you're looking for. So in any dating scenario, there are huge possibilities for you and the person who has agreed to join you.

Before you ever go on a first date you must look at it with the mentality of the glass is half full, no matter what. This will send zounds of positive chemicals to your brain allowing you to walk through those doors with far more natural confidence than you've ever had! Your date will feel that emanating from you and they'll thank you for it. If I was you, I'd be jubilated with the universe that any kind of dating interaction is happening. It really is a wonderful thing. Just take a moment to break it down a little and really think about how wonderful this opportunity is.

Someone has found you attractive! They've managed to see a glimmer of something so great about your personality they are willing to give you their time, even if it's just an hour or two. To get to know you. Wow. That's actually kinda cool.

So don't dread it! Instead, always see it as a fresh new experience with a great amplitude of positive opportunities that have so many doors. Doors with the possibility to go to any place you wish. Doors with openings to an amazing future, doors that swing open to a great friendship. Doors with openings to learn so much, just from one simple interaction. No matter the outcome you'll always learn something about yourself when you go on a date. Head over to this date with nothing but those thoughts and build your mind into a place where you'll always be looking forward to the first date and never backward.

You might have been unlucky to deal with a few crap dates where the person just wasn't nice and ruined your opinion of what's out there. You jumped on Twitter and dropped your most cynical, pulpy, and slightly funny tweet admonishing the opposite sex. But you have to go through it. You can't make an omelet without cracking some eggs. Sorry peeps.

Before you even show up to that first date you have to affirm within yourself that no matter what happens you commit to trying to have a fun experience and you will learn about yourself regardless. Always tell yourself that. It's amazing how that complete mind shift can make for an exciting first date! People can always see what's in your heart by how you behave. How you behave show's how you feel. I could go in circles but you get my point.

I'll never forget the story this one guy told me in one of my focus groups. He told me that one day he woke up and had a crazy thought. *"What if I didn't vocalize one negative sentence today"*. The results were incredible, he recounted. The thing is, this man was right. You should have seen the look of wonder and amazement on his face as he outlined the story. I believed him and I alone felt positive just from this experience he shared. He tried it for one day and he mentioned how happy he felt and how it affected his whole week. Then he said he applied it to his dating. Meaning he didn't think or vocalize one negative thing about his dates even if the date didn't go in his favor. Some other people in the group were a little skeptical and chastised him a bit, even going as far as to call him a "discount Tony Robbins". But he was honest, he let them know that it was hard at first. But with repetition and a strong mindset, anyone could do it. The room was silenced for a few seconds. Then he proceeded to share a few more sentences of this philosophy, the air was the thinnest it had been the whole meeting.

People believed him.

After we all left the meeting. I thought a lot about that story and dating in general. You see, dating isn't just about boy meets girl. Girl meets boy. It reaches and transcends the basics of human-to-human interaction. Because you're searching outside of yourself and you're looking for something with someone who isn't you. But in order to truly search and find what's right externally, you should always be working on the internal. It's about examining yourself, bettering who you are, and learning along the way. You need to look at it as an existential experience that will change your life.

I get it, you can only divulge and regurgitate why you're in the job you're in and why you live where you live and all your dogs and their names so much. Those same pieces of "getting to know you" questions get old really quickly and quite frankly tiresome. But remember, this could be it, this could be the one. You just never really know, so get excited! And be prepared for a nice healthy mutual connection. That's all you're really looking for, it's so very simple. Besides it's 2022, your dating parameters are larger than they've ever been before and we have the internet. Be of good courage!

Take into consideration, however, there are a decent number of people out there that you could easily be compatible with within your lifetime. So don't write people off so quickly. If you are serious about finding a life partner/relationship/marriage take it slow and thorough.

But don't let this ruin the expectations. Don't jump right into the future, house, cars, kids, 401ks, and all that nonsense. That's not what's going to get the job done and it will freak the other person out. Just have that outlook that glides in the air and does not dive bomb from the sky. Take everything as it comes. Be present and at the moment with that person and enjoy the small things that accumulate to you making big decisions later down the line.

Be careful how much emphasis you place on the fact that it could be the last date, though. Even though that's an ideology in the back of your mind you gotta relax and not allow that sense of optimism to delay what's going on right then within the date! Having a great sense of that unbridled optimism just means you can get excited and allow that enthusiasm to infectiously fire up the tenacity of the first date. Oh my god, they'll love it. But remember if they don't then they might not be for you and it wasn't meant to be.

Remind yourself that it's only one evening/afternoon, and then just relax and let go. Even if the sparks ultimately aren't there, the night's not a wash. You'll probably come away with new insight into your personality. Perhaps an interesting story to add to your repertoire. You can always gain something from a first date.

I'm telling you first dates really have huge opportunities. So long as you've done the necessary vetting process beforehand and your due diligence the possibilities could really be endless, so long as you finish this book the idea is that you have the best possible start, so you can finish strong. You have so much more to gain and nothing to lose, I'm gonna repeat that sentence throughout the book until it drums into your head. A new partner, an awesome friend, a wife/husband, a longtime girlfriend/boyfriend. It can bloom into something you really didn't see coming but you have to go in with that positive mindset that this truly is and will be the case.

You'd be amazed at the type of reality your mind can create if you are constantly trying to train it and put yourself in that psychological state. The very worst thing I can see happening is there's no attraction but there's pleasant conversation. Yes, you can get the sex pests, the creeps the stage 5 clingers, and all that other nonsense. But all of this is merely mental strength training for you until you meet that wonderful person. These days you have to get through all the garbage to find your diamond in the rough, there's no way to avoid that especially in 2022. You're clay who is being molded into that perfect sculpture for the people that actually matter. The more dates you go on if you genuinely try and learn you'll get better and better at finding out who you are and what you truly want.

"This could be them", please carry that mindset. Haters will say all kinds of nonsense to this. Remember misery loves company. So pay those negative, no date having losers no mind.

Haters -

- "You're trying too hard"

- "This is just a trash date"

- "Negativity, negativity, blah, blah, blah"

- (insert) funny meme to refute positivity

- "Easy for you to say"

- "This won't work for me"

- "The dating pool is full of desperados"

- "I can't expect much"

- "It's just the same old, same old"

- "Dating sucks"

- "Well I'm waiting for someone to prove me wrong"

You can guess my retort to that. It's a four-letter word if used eloquently can have a lovely effect. Then I'll follow that up with the word "off"

If you truly do not believe that sentiment of "This could be my last first date", why give that person the time of day? Why waste time meeting with someone where you don't believe it might be your last first date? Either way, the positives that I listed previously could never be time wasted but a fulfilling and enriching experience where you will always have something to take away and apply it to the next date, good or bad. What you speak will eventually come into existence. What you resist will persist. I could go on with the platitudes but I won't. What I will say is this.

This could be your last, first date.

The beauty and poetry of the first date will always lie in the attempt and effort you make on your side, it should always be the best. The very best. No matter how many first dates you go on. You should be focused on being the best version of who you are. The effort to imprint a positive experience on someone, to make their day better, to leave an encouraging mark on the dating community, and to be part of the solution, not the problem. There's just so much crap in the dating pool these days. There's also so much damn good! If you get out there with the best intentions and hope to find someone special, I promise you the universe will work with you and make it so! You can't control how the other person thinks or behaves, but you can control your behavior. So make it expectant for the best outcome. It will be infectious I tell you!

But you must be patient, this type of mindset will take some getting used to and a great length of time. So even if you feel like it's not working. Don't give up, your time will come I promise. Unfortunately, like anything else, in order to see real results, you have to keep at it. Consistency is the mother of all learning.

7. Dress Up And Make Sure People Stare!

"Dress shabbily and they remember the dress; dress impeccably and they remember the woman." —**Coco Chanel**

I promise you right now as god as my witness, your Crocs and socks will not cut the mustard for this date. Nor will your cute lululemon yoga pants and tank top. At least not on a first date anyway. I'll side with women a bit on this one. I've heard more stories from them about men who have just shown up with bootcut basic jeans, sneakers, and a crew-cut t-shirt. Not the worst thing in the world but also not a good first impression. Imagine spending 20 - 40 minutes putting on makeup and trying on different outfits and generally going out of your way to look good for someone. Then they show up with cargo shorts, flip flops, and a Panic at the Disco t-shirt. Men, if you're reading take note. Trust me a large majority of women out there make an effort on their outfits and so should you. You might be reading this thinking, "It's who I am Trey, give me a break". Making a poor effort of what you wear isn't who you are. It's who you have allowed yourself to become. Step it up! Try something new. Women like men who dress well. I've never met a lady who has explained to me how much she loves a guy who dresses like he just got out of bed. Never happened. Never will.

Remember the whole premise of this book is literally about making a good first impression and as we know the first thing people usually judge you on is appearance, make peace with that, get over it and move on. Cause that's how it is. It's never going to change.

So why would you not want to get that right? When you have a strong attraction to someone, having an engaging conversation is the next inevitable step. Just think about it, who would you be interested in speaking to if you were at a dating mixer? The person who is in baggy sweatpants and an unkempt t-shirt with the ketchup stains. Or someone who has a suit on with stylish shoes and a nice haircut. Or the person who has a nice cocktail dress, cute shoes, and a hairstyle that puts Jennifer Aniston to shame. Or the person who's wearing a hoodie, yoga pants, and Nike shoes. You have to politely remind yourself that this in fact could very well be your first, last date! How would you want to look back on the first date with your future partner or spouse? Exactly! The best thing about dressing up for a date is it's all in your control. That's one part of the date that works very well in your favor. So make the right decisions and make sure they'll never forget what you wore on that first date. You want jaws dropping and eyes fixated, and interest at its very peak. Hell, you even want the dogs to be curious.

Professor Frank Bernieri of Oregon state developed something called a "slicing methodology". It means we make a very quick assessment and judgment on someone after just a few seconds of meeting! If you've ever been in a situation where a friend of yours has brought one of their friends to a house party. Upon shaking their hands and having a few sentences you've already made your judgment on them. That's slicing! Or if you're in line to use the ATM and someone behind you gives you the willies so you cover the dial pad as you type in digits. All slicing with a slither of unconscious bias. Based on our social experiences and interactions all throughout our lives it's training us to make snap judgments instantly.

Let's go deeper though. There was a study conducted by The American Journal of Medicine. They wanted to study the attire of doctors and if that had an immediate effect on their patients' trust and confidence in the doctor. The results were a given but it was still a cool little experiment. The results essentially outlined that a doctor who dresses in a white doctor's coat and professional attire influenced how the patients saw them.

This isn't just applicable to doctors, it's all of us too. Just the way the human mind works.

You want people to stare at you when you walk in and stare at you when you walk out and have that visual stimulus that you could be the one. You look that freaking good. I can't handle it when someone shows up for a date looking like a dog's dinner. Men and women must make an effort on the first date, add some extra excitement to it! Wear something that makes you feel like the sexiest lady in the room or the most handsome bachelor in the bar, whatever makes you feel good and your best presented. Wear it and wear it well.

If you're ever unsure of what to wear, always go with smart casual. It's far better to be overdressed than underdressed. What would you rather? Flip flops and cargo pants with a billabong shirt at a fancy dessert location? Or some nice jeans and a polo shirt with some desert shoes. Summer dress and ballerina shoes to walk in the park. Or sneakers yoga pants and a hoodie. Trust me on this, men and women appreciate it when the person makes an effort. At the same time don't be an idiot. Please do not show up to the hiking date wearing wedges and a pencil skirt. Oh be wise, is there anything more I can say?

I guess you could say this...

"They need to just accept me as me, this is the package and if they don't like it, then I don't like them".

Yeah, most people who say that are single AF. It's all good I get where you're coming from, sincerely I do. But take this into consideration. Before your lovely lips even utter another sentence. Before they hear that lovely and most eloquent voice you have. They will undoubtedly be judging how you look and how you present yourself. When you shut the door to your car and walk towards them. As you rise from your seat to shake their hand and introduce yourself, as soon as you walk into that coffee shop's doorway. These are all potential moments your date is going to be judging how you look. So whatever you do make sure they're thinking, "Oh wow", not "oh no! What happened!?". You can do this! Swallow up the pride you might have and make it happen. I know your personality is warm and fuzzy and your mum loves you. But that's already in the package, we know that. Just make a little effort with your wrapping paper. You don't want to be merely liked by your date, you want to be desired, too.

> *"If you can't be better than your competition, just dress better."* – **Anna Wintour**

Your date will appreciate it.

So go out, buy an outfit and get yourself presentable. You only have one chance to make a first impression so make it impeccably memorable. I can tell you right now, I remember my first dates with people who make more of a presentation effort than those who don't. Maybe that makes me super vapid but I won't apologize for it. I like someone that looks good. It's etched in my memory and adds to one of the many reasons why I might be fond of them.

No matter what any person tells you. Allow me to give this

frank piece of information.

Looks do matter and so does your appearance. (At first)

I know. You could be a little angry listening or reading this. "True beauty is on the inside" right? Yeah, it's true. To a point. But on the first date appearance and looks are really what gets the fires initially set. Were this not true, why do you think online dating is so popular? Because it's visual. Like it or not we're very visual creatures now, more than we ever have been. People do not typically start an initial attraction because of how good the conversation is going. Sure it happens but not every time. For now, your most immediate and quickly rewarding return on investment will be your appearance. Here's the best part about that. It has nothing to do with anything but what you're wearing so you can get an awesome outfit. Check out Pinterest and type in outfit ideas, GQ, Cosmopolitan, fashion blogs. It's all there. You just have to sit your arse down and do the research. I promise you again, the same Nike Air Max sneakers you've been wearing for 5 years will not hit the spot. Maybe for your dad. But not you.

Another added bonus to a good appearance is looking after yourself physically. Again a lot of us battle with this. But the reality is, if you take your physical health and appearance seriously, your dating results will change. Deep down you know it and I know it. So do yourself a favor, stop making excuses and go for that walk, get a gym membership, don't always eat sugar, and be conscious of what you're throwing in your mouth. I hate that it's like this sometimes, but that's how we are biologically wired as humans; we can't help what we're attracted to. Good-looking, in shape and well-groomed humans are what we like. Besides, we judge everyone every time everywhere. Consciously or subconsciously. No matter how nice that person may seem on the first date, judging you is exactly what they're doing. You really do have to come at peace with that. This happens every day, when we go to work, gym, elevator, grocery store, gas station, and so forth. Everywhere you go someone will be looking at your appearance. So on the first date, give yourself the greatest possible opportunity and get it right.

One of the things I really like about dressing up for the date is that it's an absolutely confidence builder. If you have the right outfit you're going to feel like you're cock of the walk, queen of the castle, and top of the hill. Trust me, you know as well as I do that look you give yourself in the mirror when you realize you may have put together that outfit! You know, THAT OUTFIT!

If you can take courage with that alone this should allow you an extra layer of steady "self-love" fortitude. You need to kick those nerves into the dust and let that person know how awesome you are. Don't worry I'm not saying you should completely remove your own sense of style and rob the look from GQ or Cosmo. No, what I'm saying is your look should be a helpful mix of contemporary style, your own individual style, and maybe, just maybe you try a small hint of something new. You could end up loving it. Give yourself some credit, you can make a simple change, see what results you get, try and test outfits. The more you practice and try out new outfits the better you'll get and nailing the look you feel most comfortable with and a look you know works.

Trust me you don't have to break the bank to add a little bit of fashion or a glimmer of something you've never tried before. There are a few good places that sell clothes on-trend at a lovely price if you're a little conservative like me. You have H&M, Old Navy, Cotton On, and a couple of smaller market online stores. So cash shouldn't be too much of an issue. You can also give your closet a good rummage and see if you can find a classic, or mix a top you bought for 20 dollars with something classic in your closet the possibilities are endless. What matters is effort and people really appreciate the effort. Always.

A few things to take into consideration before making your pick or, when you've come up with your conclusion which outfit is better. The last time you wore that outfit, did it draw compliments? Were people fans? Did you get hit on? Did your co-workers admire it? The random lady at the gas station said something? Your frenemy at work even said your blouse looks amazing? Take all those into consideration and more. My rule is quite simple, even if there is a shred of doubt with the outfit try on another till your gut is screaming inside and banging your belly like an African drum. Yes, yes, YASSSSS! This is the one.

"My date is gonna love me in this" When you feel like that get the hell out there and go wow them!

Make those people stare.

In Summary:

    A. Research outfit ideas
    B. Mix and match old style with new style
    C. Looks and appearances do matter (Initially)
    D. You have one chance at a good first impression
    E. Wear what makes you feel good

Try this:

-    Hop on Pinterest and type in something like, "first date outfits for men/women".
- Get inspired
- Keep searching till you find something you like
- See if you have that outfit or buy it online

8. Be You And Only You

"Be who you are and say what you feel, because those who mind don't matter, and those who matter don't mind."

— **Bernard M. Baruch**

The glaring and repeated mistakes people make in relationships time and time again is by thinking they need to change for the person they love or are interested in. They try to become a little different to fit the person's usual proclivity. It's sad really, but I've done it in the past and I'm sure you have to. It's okay, though. It's almost a good thing when you grow from this and think to yourself, "Damn what on god's green earth was I thinking!?"

I remember when I dated this lovely lady called Caroline. She hated curse words. Now don't get me wrong I wasn't effing and blinding and using curse words as adjectives. But every now and then I'd let one out. It really bugged her. Till one day we were driving out of town and I said,

"Fuck! I forgot to lock the door of the apartment" We were 30 minutes out! She was upset, I was annoyed about the fact she was upset with me as I felt it was a justified curse word usage. An argument ensued. 2 years later we married.

No, I'm kidding, we promptly broke up after that.

Shit.

I broke up with her because I wanted someone to accept me as my alleged potty-mouthed self. I'm not perfect and I don't expect anyone I date to be either. This is why I expect someone to still like me and admire me for who I am. Curse words and all.

When you're not yourself you can only keep it up and maintain it for so long before the real you starts slowly seeping through those cracks of omissive dishonesty. If you spend your whole life living for people's approval you'll die from their rejection. Just be you from the get-go!

The single most attractive thing anyone can do is be themselves and be very confident in that. It's that simple Confidence + You = dating success

You know, I almost hate typing that up. Lord knows how many times people have just said, "Be yourself". But it's true. There's a reason why it's a hulking cliche.

The most genuine and authentic people I know are the most successful because they're themselves and they're unapologetic about it, they use their own moral compass as their guiding light as opposed to anyone but themselves. Go look at yourself in the mirror and give yourself a gentle reminder of who the hell you are. For example,

Joe: I'm Joe Mitchell, I'm successful, I love my mum, pay my taxes, kick-ass at work and I'm a great listener!

Hey if you're like Joe. Go do it! You jump in front of that mirror and remind yourself why you're dope as hell and anyone would be glad to have a slice of your pie. Don't believe me?

Think this is lame. Go try it right now.

Right now!

If you do this before every date the results will speak for themselves.

There's a clear difference between being your best self and being someone completely different from who you really are. For example, I hate Parks and Rec, yeah I know most millennials love that show. I'm more of a Friends guy. If my date says she loves P&R I'll say something like, "I've seen a few episodes I just can't quite get into it". I'm not being dishonest, I'm admitting I'm not a fan. You see there are subtle ways of disagreeing without being a prick. You don't want to make someone feel shitty because they don't like the same shows as you. Instead, if you turned around and said, "God that show is shit! I can't stand the acting, and Amy Poehler! God does she suck". That's ... a bit too honest. It's all about your approach and delivery. Be you but be your best you.

I do something really weird, I like to listen to show tunes. A lot. Now for most guys in their late 20's and early 30's it's not the manly thing to admit to. There's still a muddy stigma around every societal dynamic that likes to dictate what men and women should be into. I on the other hand couldn't give a monkeys. So when a woman asks me what one of my favorite albums is I'll respond authentically. A bit of Drake, a bit of Usher, and then bam!! Les Miserables. Sure there's a couple of other blokes that dig Les Mis but we're a rare breed. So be you, unashamedly. People are far more likely to connect to someone they feel is themselves vs someone clearly putting on a front and trying way too hard. You try hard you die-hard, baby. Simple as that.

I've done this and I've seen this. Some men and women will do so much just to get the person to like them. Don't do it! Just be you. But not ordinary you, your best you. For the life of me, I have no understanding of why more people are not themselves. Your siblings love you, your friends love you right? So why wouldn't that person? You're a likable human being I promise and hey even if your … kind of an asshole, some people like that too. There really is someone out there for everyone. You won't find that out if you're a very cunning wolf sliding in and out of that fancy sheep's clothing you own. I understand, we don't want to be turned away for who we truly are. We don't want to just get emotionally naked with a total stranger. So what, then? You are, who you are. So show up, wear that big smile and go and have fun! That's really the only way it should be in my opinion. Anything else would be robbing them of the true and full experience of you and how wonderful you are.

You have to run in there like a football player onto a field, you're confident in yourself and you know your personal brand, you wear your brand and anyone who comes into contact with you knows exactly what time it is when they meet you. This should alleviate any slight (or major) pressure you might have. Then they'll love how piercingly veritable you are. It's a tricky situation because essentially you should care about the initial meeting, but shouldn't worry about the outcome. That way it will be far easier to relax and be yourself.

When you are truly comfortable in your own skin. you're able to find honest common ground and it builds sturdier foundations for the future. There had to be something right? There had to be something that this person liked about you or they would never have agreed to go on a date. So just be you. Positive and real expectations about the date can only carry your eminence and translate a long-lasting representation of who you are. The idea here is that your own personality carries such weight that they leave driving away in their car thinking. Wow, what an amazing person. I can't wait to see them again! This can be realized in your life this week! If you work on what you know your biggest personality strengths are and you're able to show that. It's going to be a great experience for you every time. You'll never know more internal freedom when you release the clasps of expectation and slowly but gradually morph into who you were meant to be.

Be a free bird with a little bit of fear and with a slight determination without being a "me monster". For example, you could be in a bar and hear your favorite song. Maybe you like to sing it in the shower or on the way to work. Why not sing along with it in the bar, ask them to dance to it with you. I'm not saying to go crazy but if that matches your personality go do it!

People feed off that kind of energy! And quite frankly if it's too much for them, then get rid of them, they're not the ones. You want to be with someone who's not uptight right?

It's like anything else. Imagine you're in the shopping mall. You rarely check an item of clothing without checking the price, right? Could you imagine finding a jacket that makes your eyes pop out of your head and you know. Yes you know you're going to break necks with this jacket. But there's no price. So you walk up to the counter and you're ready to pay.

Cashier: "That would be $800.00, please.

You: "WAT!?"

Yeah, that would be insane right? So why hide your "personality price". Be your best self upfront. Simple as that. Don't hide how much your true value is. Granted you don't have to tell them your social security and why your grandad never loved you as much as your sister and all that other stuff. But behave how you would in front of one of your best friends whom you love and respect. Well, not exactly how you'd behave with your friends, something loosely around that type of interaction. Usually, when I see my buddy I say, "Well, well who let your ass in here".

Don't welcome your date that way!

So remember, you want them to see the price head-on. Look at it this way, what would you be happy telling a practical stranger at a bus stop? If you were having a little chat. What would you tell them? Keep it that level and elevate in notches as you so please and when you feel the most comfortable and you both are in the attraction zone.

I remember in college when I was interested in this very attractive woman in my psychology class. Before the class would start for those of us who were early we'd always have a little chat. Whenever I would speak to her I would brag about getting drunk and how much I loved to party. She wasn't impressed or remotely interested. Then I tried to drop humble brags about my football team accomplishments. Still nothing.

Until one day she started small talk as always she asked how my night was. I told her I was finishing off a book called Anna Karenina. Her jaw dropped and she immediately lit up with conversations about the book, then we spoke about other books we both read. We dated for about 6 months after that. My point here is that being who you are and being vocal with your truth is the best way.

Say who you are, from the start. That way there are no surprises for them and they'll fall for your rich and desirable personality. But it really is the most valuable thing you can do on the first date. If they don't like it, fine. Remember it's all part of the package. So what that means for you is this. You probably shouldn't even entertain the thought of, "I wonder what kind of person they're attracted to". That will only hurt your confidence to be comfortable in your own skin for the first date, trust me. When you're yourself their decision is very black and white and straightforward. They either like it or they don't. You find out interest levels expediently. You can't get a better result than that!

Remember:

A. Who you are is actually incredible
B. There's someone for everyone
C. Be you with respect to who they are
D. Be the person your family loves
E. Never hide your personality, "price". Eventually, they'll find out
F. You can't keep up the lie forever
G. Being confident in who you are building a better foundation of trust
H. Being who you were truly meant to be is the ultimate source of inner freedom
I. Never ask yourself what kind of person they're attracted to

Try This:

- Think about a guilty pleasure or something most people don't know about you. Be ready to share it when the opportunity presents itself

9. Check In

Some people out there are dating pros. I'm serious, some people will ask thought-provoking questions. Questions that really make you look into yourself. You can get into some pretty deep philosophical and hypothetical conversations on a first date. Nothing wrong with that at all. But add some genuine check-ins. "How was your day?" "How was work?" Yeah, it's the first date and you aren't too familiar with each other. But it makes people feel a little more at ease and more comfortable. Before you start rifling through the conciliatory date questions. Let them know you're a real person who sees them as more than a picture in a dating app or some stranger you met through a friend or at a bar. What I like to do sometimes is figure out halfway through the date how interested someone really is as time goes but just to see if we're on the same page and I know I can enjoy their company further.

> If you're having a good conversation but it's only contingent on all of the good questions you ask and you're driving the conversation. It doesn't mean they're not fully interested but start looking out for some of their responses and see if they're being as thoughtful with their questions. If they don't really ask you too many questions, if any, about you. They're probably not as interested. And even if they are, what kind of person wants to spend more time with someone who's so self-centered they can't even see that maybe they should try and get to know the

other person too.

Now I'm not one for playing games, trust me. But at the same time, you gotta know how interested the person is. So there are different ways you can gauge this when you're with them.

Here's the first thing you can do to check in to see how much they enjoy spending time with you and if they want to do this again. Try these where you're at the 45 to 60-minute mark.

> A. Whether you're at the movies, having a nice stroll in the park, eating ice cream, or enjoying a round of drinks with them. When you do this as I mentioned, try it at the one-hour mark. Something like, oh goodness it's 8:00!? Or, "oh it's been an hour". They'd probably respond with something like, "Oh do you have somewhere you have to be?". Remain cool, calm, and collected and just say something like, "Oh no, just didn't realize the time went by so quickly" This is where you have to be super vigilant and self-aware. If they seem like they agree and have been so into the conversation, Great (You read their body language, eye contact, vocal intonation) they could agree and make a comment about the good conversation. By then you have a breath of understanding with their level of interest.
>
> B.   A Small Touch

Touch is one of those things that gives you another check-in scenario where you can feel how much they're comfortable and understand how much they enjoy spending time with you. Now don't get me wrong if you first meet them at the venue of choice and they aren't quite a big hugger as much as you are. Don't read into it, they just met you for goodness sake! But after a good 45 to 60 minutes. Try and go in for some very light non-creepy touching. Now I know what you're thinking, "I don't want to creepily touch them without consent throughout the date to make sure they're interested". It's not like that at all. You actually might be doing it more subconsciously than you think. But for education's sake let's go through some scenarios when you can lightly touch and won't get sent to jail.

From what I hear, jail ain't Disneyland.

The first interaction can be the same as referenced above. A small hug, who doesn't like hugs. A small and quick hug isn't invasive, not over the top, or aggressive. To be honest it's my personal view that if someone is against a small church hug (Quick, hug two pats on the upper back) at the beginning of a date, they need to loosen up a bit and relax. There's a clear difference between hugging a total stranger or hugging someone you've planned and scheduled time to be with. So hug them!

The 2nd can be laughing at a funny joke and patting them lightly on the side of the upper shoulder. Or giving them a gentle double pat on the leg. Even a small handshake is contact. Now here's where it gets exciting. If they start doing the same thing to you, THEY LIKE YOU. It's amazing. If done right and the dating harmony is succinct, not only will they start mirroring those actions back, but they might slowly start inching a little closer to you. But a word of warning, please, please be smart about how you do this. Don't start grabbing every piece of their body slowly throughout the night as there's a very large chance that the only person that will be touching you back, will have a badge and a gun. The next date you have after that will be with someone in the same prison cell. Trust me, they'll be touching you too.

Just be respectful and do it with some smoothness, right? If you're in a bar with air conditioning much like Narnia. Look at her arm, exclaiming that she has goosebumps, and politely ask her if you can put her jacket back on. Or if there's a piece of fluff in his hair just grab it out then tidy up his hair after the fact. These are very small things but it just builds up the light sexual tension to a nice pace. It also allows you to see engagement and interest level to a point where you have fairly concrete answers.

Remember

1. Mention how much your enjoying yourself and check for a response

2. Ask them how they're genuinely feeling

3. Try some light consensual non-threatening touching

10. Get To The Passions.

"I have no special talents. I am only passionately curious." **Albert Einstein**

You know what people like more than ever. Themselves. I'm serious, not in a negative way, but most people like talking about themselves. It's not a bad thing, it's just how most of us are wired. So figure out what some of their deepest passions are. It could be something like this. "So after work, you're relaxing and doing something you love, what is it?" When this happens in most cases they'll be polite and say something like. "I love going on hikes" or "I love painting" and "Reading a lot of books". This is where you dig a little deeper. You turn around and say, "Awesome, what do you like about it?" then they'll open up (Hopefully) and you'll see a completely different side to them. Their face will grow animated, their speech more freely flowed and their intensity increased just subtly. This is what you want. Sure most people have a 9-5, that's all good. But chances are they've just gotten done with that for the day or for the weekend, talk about anything but their job and watch them come alive. If they respond with something like, "Nothing really". That's your first red flag in my opinion. Who wants to date someone with no hobbies or passions? Outside of work, not me. You shouldn't either. Don't get me wrong, if someone's a doctor or a lawyer saving lives in the court and in the hospital. Fine, you can let them go on about their job, but if someone works as a project manager at the same company for 8 years. No, just no.

Get them to talk about the topic that interests them the most. Like I said you want to smoothly dig around them until you find the treasure that makes them come completely alive with excitement. That positive emotion they feel will be associated with you! Because you're the kind of person that can bring it out of them. Wouldn't that be amazing! You can do it. With scintillating humor and an open mind, you can really find joy in someone being completely jubilated over what they love the most. The more you do this it will stretch your selfless muscles just a little and you'll be used to hearing that person out first before you start piping up about yourself.

Remember the vibe of the conversation you have is always going to be far more important than the actual content sometimes. If you're genuine and real about really trying to see and learn the things they love. I promise you the conversation will be so bright and seamless. If you've done it correctly you should expect some marvelous reciprocity between you and your date. If not, then jog on and jog fast! Even if things get a little personal or political. If you're going in with litmus tests and axes to grind, it probably won't go as well.

And if you can't quite get to the passions they love, ask them questions that most people love to answer.

Questions about them!

Remember people looooove talking about themselves and if they're truly a nice considerate person. Them asking you about yourself will just be a natural consequence. Easier said than done right. Spice things up a bit.

Rather than:

You: **"So what do you do for work?"**

Instead, it should be, **"What's the best part of your job?"**

Ahhhh. Ahhhh? You're starting to get it now, right? Just try and glide through understanding their passions.

Be careful about those corny questions like, "If you could have any superpower, what would it be? They're not bad questions per se. They're just soooo forced. Avoid those corny "job interview' questions.

Example: "So um, what's your 5 year plan?"

Yuck! I cringe typing that up. These people out there exist. I've been asked that many times before.

This goes for lots of social interactions: ask a lot of questions, and make them less about "testing" people than about genuinely finding out what they have to say.

What you want to do is get to the whys of their how's and the how's of their whys. So when they tell you how they got into the medical field. You say, "That's really cool, why did you decide that was the career for you?"

When they give you the "how" of getting to the state they live in now you say. "Why did you want to move to California?"

When they discuss how they came to find the boxing studio down the street through that friend of theirs. You ask, "why do you love boxing so much?" What's the best part of boxing for you?

Getting to the why's allows a different layer of the conversation to really explore that mental stimulation between the two of you. Further widening the opportunity for the both of you to really connect. It's about helping each other to feel emotion. Allowing someone to express what they're passionate about is such a heavy emotional punch. Getting to why's and how's can enable both of you to feel, based on the answers you give and receive. You're trying to evoke emotion from both of you so a sincere human experience can take its root just by having a good first date.

Some of the worst dating experiences I've ever had have been as a result of my mind not really being present there. I didn't quite stop thinking about work or what I had going on the next day. Maybe you're thinking about how terrible the last date was or perhaps how your luck has been bad all year when it comes to dating. Don't do it! Be focused on your date.

Neither of you knows how the night will go. But it's way better if you're there to get to the roots of why they're so passionate about their hobbies and build strong blueprints to start creating something real and healthy.

> *"To succeed you have to believe in something with such passion that it becomes a reality."*

- **Anita Roddick**

Believe in your romantic future with such a passion. Such a rich conviction that you know, when you connect with someone. Your romantic future is one conversation away.

11. You Don't Have To Be Anywhere You Don't Want To.

"When we fail to set boundaries and hold people accountable, we feel used and mistreated." ~ **Brené Brown**

Time is one of the most valuable commodities anyone has if not the most valuable, most products you buy these days, and the commercials you watch are about saving time, making time, getting time back. So if you're going on a date with someone, especially a 1st date. Remember you can dip whenever the hell you want. Yeah, I said it. Now don't get me wrong. Don't be a classless nincompoop and leave after 5 minutes. But there are circumstances where I would suggest leaving in 30 minutes. You're well within your rights to do that. That's why I'm always strongly against meeting at someone's house for the first date. There are some pretty obvious red flags as to when you should leave early.

What are those? Do you ask? As always I'll give you some examples.

A. Continuously unwanted sexual advances.

For example this:

Her: "Yeah I just got a new swimsuit for my trip to San Diego, next week.

Him: "Yeah? I bet your boobs look great in that swimsuit. Make sure you send me a pic"

Not the worst right? Cringeworthy and a little inappropriate, but not the worst. Hell, some people may even be into that. The fact is it's a little bit too forward. But what if they continue.

Her: "Yeah when I run in the morning it's a little hard as it's really cold around this time of year"

Him: "Do you like it?"

Her: "Like what?"

Him: "Like it cold"

Her: "Well no, that's why I... don't run..."

Him: "I thought you'd like it when it's cold and people can see you"

Her: "What?"

Him: "Heh, heh. You know. Your nipples show, don't women love to show shit like that"

Her: "......."

Him: "I mean, I'm only kidding"

Again this isn't crime watch or America's most wanted. But it's borderline harassment if not actual harassment. But I get it some women are very nice and might still sit through it. But what about this;

Her: "Yeah I usually don't kiss on the first date"

Him: "Oh we might be doing a little more than a kiss..."

This is a true story by the way. Red flag, abort the mission, run!

Get out of the house, leave and just scoot.

I say if you can get away, obviously do it in a respectful way but just be honest. Why waste each other's time? Sure it's going to hurt their ego a little but they'll get over it. I'm sure you've hurt someone far worse by just ignoring their text or vanishing from their lives. So learn how to do it respectfully but on a date. If you feel physically threatened then there are other ways you can go. I'll get to that in a few chapters later.

Some people are brutal though. I had a friend who met this guy on a date and he was significantly shorter than his profile had suggested, in addition to that he was very much 70 pounds bigger. Yeah, apparently this guy was the ultimate catfish, the lord emperor lizard king of Catfishes. You wanna know what she did?

After about 15 minutes of entertaining small talk about his BMW, she politely said.

"I'm sorry. This may come as rude, but this just isn't working for me. Do you mind if I leave?". Haha haha, can you believe that!? Brutal! But it was effective. As I'm writing this I'm still laughing. Haha, you imagine the look on that poor guy's face. But hey it was a headshot! a quick finish. He had no one to blame but himself for being dishonest. If I was that guy I'd dust my shoulders, walk it off and think to myself, "Well I'm not everyone's type". Furthermore, if I was him I might think, "Mmm I should update those photos and not lie about my age, height, or weight."

I get it though, our world is based on having the appearance of being likable and wanting to be seen as a nice person. So much so that a lot of people care far more about how they're perceived as opposed to who they actually are. I say, fuck it. If you don't like the date. Leave, why waste your time. Yet so many people want to "see the date out". Or they want to be polite. Not a bad thing, but guess what, you can in fact be polite and still leave the date early. Don't be a people pleaser, especially for someone you don't know from Adam. In fact, don't be a date pleaser, if the date is barely bearable just go. Be a YOU pleaser. At least on the first date. But at the same time give the person a chance. I would only say leave a little early if you feel like:

- They're very inappropriate
- Racist, homophobic and sexist comments
- You feel threatened
- They're very aggressive
- They're very argumentative
- They smell really, really bad

I'll hit you up with a few tips to escape the terrible date.

    A.   Know all routes to each exit

I'm not the biggest fan of flying, traveling in general, to be honest. But what I really abhor is the obligatory "exits" intro about safety and what you should do if the plane crashes. Man, I don't care. I just want to get to Mexico, baby! Danger be damned! I'll deal with that later. But when it comes to a bad date, you gotta have a quick, polite, and easy escape plan. For example, a basketball game, jazz concert, or even a theme park might sound all good for a first date.

Perhaps someone's wooing you to your heart's content and making a huge concentrated effort. But what if they're boring as hell. Do you wanna be stuck in a 2-hour event with someone who is headbanging dull? Someone so boring it makes you want to jump off a short pier. Yuck, sounds like Dante's 7th circle of hell. Don't accept those plans. Rather, just be honest and say, "I usually like to do something a little low-key for a first date if that's okay with you. Boom there you go one hour, low-key date for drinks. Never fails. If you're a lady and through the date, you're realizing it's going nowhere. Pay for your own drinks. Don't give this guy another reason to pursue you. It's not bad to allow a gentleman to pay. But don't assume he understands social norms. For most men when you let them pay, in the back of their minds there must be some interest.

B. Try some honesty (It's an odd notion these days but what's the worst that could happen)

I'm telling you it's crazy how people totally like honesty. All you have to do is just say, it's been nice meeting you but it might be better if we're friends, shake a hand, and then biggity bounce. If they get in a huff and puff and tell you how much of a horrible person you are. There's your confirmation that they were indeed, the turd sandwich you thought they were. And trust me, if you're too honest in telling them why. It only makes them beg and plead as to why they're such a good fit for you. You tell them exactly why the first thing they're going to do is to list all the reasons why you're wrong and you're totally right for them. They'll just come up with rebuttal after rebuttal. So I would save them the raw direct response. Merely respond with this sentence. "I just don't think we'd be compatible". That's pretty honest, now leave. You don't owe anyone an essay or an explanation, especially on a first date. I mean, when you're in court to a freaking judge you can say, "I plead the fifth". So why would you spend time explaining to a hapless sucker who just doesn't get it? Make like a tree and leave.

C. Okay fine, then go lie!

If you feel that being honest is rude. You can always go the chicken route and lie. Yeah, it's a pretty raw move but you want to "spaaare their feelings" right? Just have a little preplan with your friend. Have them call you at the 30-minute mark and then make up a reason why you have to leave. Perfect deviousness to the fullest. Muahahahaha. I think this is a little bit of a weak move and won't do anything for strengthening your muscles to dispense rejection at a whim. But if the person really is making you feel pretty shitty and uncomfortable then you gotta go with it. That's the only way they'll learn never to do it again. Essentially you'll be saving someone else's time by just leaving and hitting them where it hurts.

12. Tripping On A Sidewalk Doesn't Mean You'll Never Walk Again.

"No matter what life throws at you, don't become jaded or cynical. Love is worth the risk."

— **Wayne Gerard Trotman**

Look, bad dates happen, there's no way around it. That's just how it is. Sorry.

But don't worry, the chances of you going for 2 for 2 or 5 for 5 bad dates are highly unlikely. That's just not how dating goes. Now, let's say you are **10 for 10** with bad dates. This one might take some self-reflection. Apologies. It might not be an issue of the other person. Yes it's true, I think to some degree it's a question of people clicking, but sometimes there are internal issues you might not be aware of. It's important to ask your friend, a real friend! What do they think? If you're 10 for 10 and upwards with terrible dating experiences. Ask your friends a few real questions:

Question 1: "Hey if you could pick one opportunity for me to personally improve, what would it be?"

Question 2: "What shitty things do I do That you think I should change?"

Question 3: "Is there anything better I could be doing on my first dates?"

Question 4: "Dude I suck at first dates, you got any tips?"

You get the main gist, right? It doesn't have to be these questions verbatim but the idea is that you're humble enough to ask a trustworthy friend for some advice. I'll forewarn you, this is gonna hurt. Most people don't have frank conversations with their friends like this. So you probably won't like what you're going to hear. If you don't have any friends, jump on Reddit for advice or a youtube guru's and jump in their comment section. There truly are a myriad of options right at your fingertips. The most important thing is that you don't let your run of bad luck hold you back from greatness! Being the best version of yourself and sweeping that superb and marvelous person of their feet is in reach. I understand, I promise. It's hard to put yourself out there on a first date, but it's also kinda hard to put yourself out there with your friends.

Be vulnerable, open, transparent, and say.

"I need help".

But that in itself helps you to overcome some anxiety before you meet someone on your first date. Trust me. Start doing things differently. If you want your dating life to change. You have to change, if you want things to be different, you have to do things differently. It really is that simple. No amazing, superlative and hyperbolic phrase is gonna help you to grow on the first dates you have. But the simple practice and theory of trying things out and doing things just a little differently is not only a great chance for you.

But a great change for your personal life. If you talk too much and your friends tell you so, that can be applied to life and it can change every interaction you have. Not just interactions with your date. If you're always late and your family or close friends tell you that, but then all of a sudden you learn to be punctual. This affects your personal life first and then seeps into your dating life.

Basically, if you keep having shit dates, change it up and change your life! Because it won't just be your changing things for dating's sake. It will be you changing things for a better future!

But remember metaphorically speaking, if you trip over a curb on a sidewalk are you really not going to walk the sidewalk again? Hell no! If anyone told you this you'd think they were certifiably insane. So why would you apply that same logic to dating? One bad date? Then you're out there shaking your fists at the highest mountain top swearing off the opposite sex. C'mon, you know it's not that bad. Your time will come! You have to be incredibly patient and learn from your mistakes. Create your own moral dating code of conduct and stick to it. Your true love is out there. Just gotta put yourself in the dating sphere and stick with the process. The best thing is, you probably have an abundance of people out there who could be your true love!

When you go on a first date, it's always important to have your wits about you. But keep some of your expectations in a cage for the night and just roll with the punches. I like to go there with the most open mind and not allow previous romantic atrocities to ruin my first date. Be present and just have a good time, I know it's a thought you've heard many times. But let loose, extinguish those fears, and have at it. I have a good idea of what you might be thinking already or have done so in the past when it comes to first dates.

Are they really my type, what height do I remember him as, is she a fickle, does she care about what job I have, is he a player, does he live with his mum. All of those things are very valid questions but I would just lay those to rest and find out for yourself. Allowing what happened in the past to dictate possible outcomes of the future is terribly nonsensical. It almost renders you helpless to the possibility of a positive outcome and puts banana peels everywhere for you before you even turn up at the venue.

Imagine if a football player had one bad game. That same night he retires, all because of a bad game. You'd nearly spit your Cheerio's out.

If you were about to box a pretty formidable opponent would you put a blindfold on and let luck decide your fate!? Hell no you wouldn't. So why oh why would you blind yourself to the possibilities of an amazing connection, by only seeing the bad dates you've had to deal with. On top of that blinding yourself from a possible dope-arse person. Think about all the opportunities you and other people have missed out on based on inflated expectations and most importantly, bad first date experiences that you've subtly allowed to alter your mindset. Therefore it slowly ruins what could have been an otherwise great date!

There are some people that wear this burden on their shoulders and carry that baggage to every date. Do not be that person! Don't force an experience for what you want, instead embrace it for what you have, right in front of you. Carry a deep-rooted and sincere value for human interaction with you to every date. Start every date with a clean paradigm, see them as they present themselves. Take as many positives away from the first date as you can and make it a habit. You owe it to yourself and your time spent to learn and grow from any romantic dating interaction. Most importantly learn and grow from bad dating interactions too.

13. It's All In The Eyes!

"Eye contact beats any conversation."

— **Christina Strigas**

Eye contact is very cool. There's something about listening intently and really looking into that person's soul figuring out what makes them, them. In their mind, they're thinking wow, this person is really listening to me and things might work out a little better. You know what I hate. Talking to someone and they're on their phone or there typing or every now and then when your date hears someone coming in the coffee shop they look up to see who it is. Be locked in with your date. They've given you their time, so be enthralled with them!

But don't do it too much. You don't want to come across as some low-rate state fair hypnotist. It might not be as effective and it could come across as if you're trying to exert far too much dominance. You gotta really figure out the right amount of intensity and balance it with how you approach eye contact. Hold that strong silent fix on that person and every now and then glance elsewhere. It's a different level and subtle connection builder that keeps you focused, engaged, and my favorite word. Present. This kind of intensity can really layer the attraction throughout the date.

"There is a saying, 'Eyes are the windows to the soul.' It means, mostly, people can see through someone else by eye contact in seven seconds. I have a habit that if I meet someone I don't know, I'd like to look at her or his eyes on purpose. When my eyes lay on them, I can immediately see their true color". - **Peng Liyuan**

It's kind of an understated art that you must develop further in terms of having a good date. You're almost listening but with your eyes. Sounds weird right? Let me break it down...

You have to carefully watch and observe their body language and eye contact and try and pick up on subtle observations you can see. Listen with your eyes. People do not know what you're thinking, never assume they do. Especially on the first date. Consider things such as. Where is their head positioned, how are they sitting, arms folded or relaxed? Hands-on the drink, hands on the table? Where do their eyes wan? rTo every new person who comes into the venue? Or solely on you? These are all things to take into consideration. When you're looking intently in their eyes it allows a different level of priority and you'll be able to understand exactly where they are coming from, you're almost forcing yourself to make sure you don't skip a beat. So that when you leave you feel like you have assessed whether this is worth another shot.

"Few realize how loud their expressions really are. Be kind with what you wordlessly say."

— *Richelle E. Goodrich,* **Making Wishes**

Holy cow! non-verbal communication is incredibly sexy for dating communication without even uttering a single sentence. You owe it to yourself to know the signs! This will enable you to be a powerful and confident distributor of amazing eye contact to those you feel like you want to have a good buzz with.

Some people convey the most information when they say nothing.

I'll give you an example, watch any James Bond movie and just watch his eye contact. Wouldn't it be nice if you could master the art of communicating verbally and non-verbally? You can! The best part is it can be catered to your personality too. There is never going to be a universal size for this, but there will be universal benefits if you practice and master this dating art form.

> *"I do listen. I just wait for the words to stop and your eyes to speak."*

— Richelle E. Goodrich, Slaying Dragons

Eye contact isn't really used that much as a powerful connection tool by most people. If it is, it's usually used by those naturally as opposed to someone trying to use it as a different level of emotional relation. There's a reason why your grandad always looked you in the eyes when he was telling you off for grabbing a slice of apple pie. He wanted to look into those eyes and discover if it was indeed you who snuck a piece before dinner (Or if it was your shithead little brother).

> *"93% of communication occurs through nonverbal behavior & tone; only 7% of communication takes place through the use of words."*

—John Stoker

Eye contact is a dying dating art form. These days most people have their eyes glued to something else. It takes away most of their attention, causes car accidents, divorces, child neglect, and people walking into a crosswalk blindly. Yes, you guessed it. It's our phones.

I've been guilty of it sometimes. People are so mind-numbingly drawn to their technology these days it's hard to hold good eye contact and develop a good connection with a lot of people, your just not used to looking at something other than your phone for such a long time. Look technology isn't bad, it's created so much good. I for one, don't know what I would do if I couldn't connect my iPhone to my car's Bluetooth. But check this little trick out.

If you have an iPhone. Go to settings, click on "screen time". Your whole perspective will change. And you'll value human interaction far better.

There are some rich benefits associated with developing and maintaining good eye contact with your date. I'll go through them and the skills you're going to learn in order to get to know your date better and give the first date another texture of romance.

The benefits are in abundance and can help you not only in your dating life but in all other aspects too. You'll build curiosity, rapport, sexual tension, wanting, trust and familiarity. But much like anything else eye contact has to have a centerpiece, a pillar, or a foundation on which you both build your house. If you can remember these you should be fine before you start learning more advanced techniques.

I'll say again, this isn't a way to trick your date into liking you or some corny Jedi mind trick. This is merely another dimension for both of you to draw some kind of romantic conclusion when the date ends. It's as simple as that. So let's get into the nitty-gritty.

Avoidance: If someone you're interested in gives you clear and direct eye contact, give it right back, this is a nice warm sign that your interaction is wanted. If you decide to avoid a decent amount of eye contact this will show that you don't really want to be there and you're not as confident. If that's the case, fine, but good luck trying to get that 2nd date. Never look down, never. Scientists have indicated that this is a sign of weakness. No one wants to date someone who is deemed weak (Sheesh, humans are brutal)

Chill: Don't scare a poor person off cause you're looking at them like a damn detective. Relax and be chilled with your eye contact. Think of it this way, your eyes and facial expression have to demonstrate and look as if you're listening intently to someone telling you the things they like about you. So here's a quick challenge. Look in the mirror, pretend someone has told you something they admire about you. Got it? Now that's the face and eyes you want when you're maintaining positive eye contact. Just relax and remember that face. Trust me, the last thing you want to do is go around mean-mugging someone you're on a date with, you don't want your face to look like you're on the front of a rap album cover. They might think you're crazy as hell. Relax those eyebrows a bit, be in the moment and give yourself a little sophisticated edge. Try and be a little bit more deliberate with that eye contact you have.

Black and White: Eye contact is a great indicator of interest because there's usually no in between. Either they are interested or not. Eye contact can demonstrate the emotion of, "come closer baby". Or, "Holy shit, I gotta get out of here!". It can cause a nice easy-going state. Or a state of great worry and apprehension. When you flirt with someone using eye contact people feel like you have a very strong character and it shows an unfettered level of confidence that can be infinite with its use.

Anger or Lust?: Tracey Cox, a columnist for The Daily Mail online laments on something called the "Four and Half Second Scan". She basically explains that any normal face scan by a man or a woman takes about 3 seconds. But if someone's interested they'll scan for 4 ½ seconds. It's an interesting theory but it holds its weight in gold. I tried it and it works. I continued to read the article and It goes on to get really spicy.

"Eye contact of more than 10 seconds between two people means one of two things: you're about to fight or have sex (well, you want to anyway). Prolonged eye contact produces intense emotional reactions regardless of whether it's a fist or a pair of lips heading your way. It activates the nervous system, raises our heart rate and blood flow, and stimulates the production of certain hormones. Just about everyone knows being watched is a sign someone's interested, so if you want to subtly make your intentions known, this is the way to do it".

That's pretty amazing when you really think about it. That's one of the many arsenals we've already discussed right at your disposal. It's free of charge and you can start doing it today! Maintain nice and steady eye contact and see the results for yourself.

Remember:

    A. Increased eye contact shows engagement and interest
    B. It slowly builds a deep intimate connection
    C. Listen with your eyes
    D. What you say is how you look
    E. If someone maintains eye contact for more than 10 seconds. It's on.

Action Item: Look in the mirror, pretend someone has told you something they admire about you. Practice that look when maintaining eye contact.

THE FIRST DATE FIX

14. Body Language

"The utmost form of respect is to give sincerely of your presence." – **Mollie Marti**

I know I know! It's such a roving cliche that is thrown around at work, at parties, and all the other good places weird humans go to socialize. But it matters and you need to work with this more. It's the part of dating that people don't pay as much attention to it as they should, much like eye contact. It's insane because body language accounts for so much of what's not being said and can add an extra edge to your first date much like eye contact.

In fact, I'd wager to say that if you worked on your eye contact or body language alone for a few weeks you'll see immediate results!

By displaying and picking up on good body language, it puts you in a better driver's seat. When you become aware and actually start experimenting with great positive and welcoming body language, the differences will be astounding. Starting with how you're perceived and the aura that comes across. People can't resist a strong bodily presence, so much so they don't even realize they're admiring it. There truly is a science to this.

You'd be surprised by what you notice when you're locked in on a first date. Body language is 55.8% of how we communicate. 55.8% percent! This stat has been around for decades yet time and time again people fail to utilize this on first dates. That's more than half of the communication. No pressure, but you need to start taking it seriously when it comes to galvanizing your potential mate.

"When the eyes say one thing, and the tongue another, a practiced person relies on the language of the first."

— **Ralph Waldo Emerson**

So what do you do? What kind of body language do you display? It's actually quite simple. The way you think and the emotions running through your brain will dictate how your body looks. If you're sad, you're going to look sad. If you're nervous you're going to look nervous. If you have moderate anxiety it's going to look like you have... you guessed it moderate anxiety. So your mindset should be relaxed and chilled. Nothing affects you because all you care about is getting to know this person and having a great time.

1. Get to know someone 2. Have a great time 3. They're interested

Prep yourself with that paradigm beforehand and I guarantee you'll have an awesome date by naturally displaying good body language. It all starts in the head. Think about this before and on the way to the date and when you get there display a natural outward body language that exudes a relaxed and welcoming nature. If you think about it before and on the way to the date the body language will be so organic. You don't know this person and they don't know you. So all your movements should be chill, relaxed, chillaxed, and very open. Making the other person feel comfortable and welcome is half of the battle. Don't get too close, but don't be too far. You want to be about a forearm length in front of them or by their side.

What most people don't understand is that the mind and body are so seamlessly connected without us even realizing it because it's so commonplace. What the mind is the body conveys, when our minds are fully engaged and enthralled in the other person, so is our body.

"Our bodies change our minds, our minds change our behaviour and our behaviour changes our outcomes". - **Amy Cuddy**

There are a few nifty tricks you can do to master body language.

Superhero Pose -

Have you ever seen a superhero movie? Where the superhero runs to the screen at the end of the movie or poses and says some corny shit like, "I'm Batman", "I'm Spiderman" and "I'm superman". Let's focus on that for a while. It's known in the body language community as the superhero pose. Before you get carried away. I don't want you running through the coffee shop pretending to fly or pretending you have a Batarang attached to your utility belt. Don't go grabbing people by the collar screaming, "where is she!". I mean you have to master some superhero poses and display some kind of positive confidence and power, but you're not trying to become a superhero. But if you feel like making some memories, show up in a Batman costume and email me your results.

The first pose is simple, whilst you're waiting in line for some Gelato or at the bowling alley or wherever you're waiting. Simply stand with your chest out put both hands on your hips and stand like a superhero. If you still don't really have a clue of what I mean google: "Superman Pose". Be superman or supergirl with one simple body language trick.

Smiling -

This one is a classic but again, some people are oblivious to it.

Just sit, with a warm smile and listen intently. I don't mean that awkward smile you see on Dancing with the Stars when they're dancing the whole time and have this creepy fixated smile on their face. That's kinda weird and creepy. But rather a warm, open, and welcoming smile that promotes understanding and romantic intent. Have your body facing them, have an open body position pointed towards them, and flash that smile when you agree with something or when you're listening. Granted if they're telling you about their dead dog, Morty. Do not sit there smiling like a Cheshire cat. If you're very much working on improving these things such as smiling, how you sit and stand. These are just small sequences you can brush up on to make sure you're the ultimate date. I know I like to say practice in the mirror a bunch. But it works I promise. It would be easy for you to be thinking in your head, "That's just not natural to me!?" Neither was going for a run. But I ran 3 times a week till it was a natural routine in my schedule and I lost 30 pounds then went to run a half marathon. Think of it this way, is it really that bad that you practice smiling in the mirror so much that it becomes a part of who you are? Nope, exactly so go and do likewise my friends.

Remember:

1. Your mind controls your body language get control of your mind before the date
2. Practice smiling in the mirror
3. Make sure you're in the zone before your date

15. Don't Be The Facebook/Snapchat/ Ig Story Person.

I considered the concept of "oversharing", and what under sharing might be, and whether it was ever possible to settle on something in between. -**David Nicholls**

We all know that person right? The man or woman on Facebook always airing their dirty laundry. Or posting their ambiguous quotes on Instagram. "You realize people aren't shit when you're down in the dumps". You know, passive-aggressive quotes like that. Or Facebook statuses like this...

FB Status A: "Why is life so shit to me I feel like I'm never gonna win"

FB Status B: "God, I wish I was never born, people keep breaking my heart, I have SO MUCH love to give! The moment you love someone they treat you like shit, f**k love!"

FB Status C: "So much for a happy birthday, found out my mum just slept with my cousin"

FB Status D: "Someone just shit on my front lawn, what's the world coming to!"

FB Status E: "Men really ain't shit. My boyfriend cheating on me with my physician".

FB Status F: "Nice to know my wife can't keep her coke addiction, sorry guys but this is the only way she'll learn, if I expose her for what she really is"

Yeah, they sound extreme but stuff like this happens online all the time. People crying out for attention, not knowing the right outlet. Instead, we either sit there laughing (Status C) or we sit there feeling sorry for the person and offer a message of happiness in their DMs. Hoping that they see it and are a little bit happier by your show of support.

Now imagine being on a date and this happens:

Him: "You seem pretty cool, I can't believe anyone would let you go"

Her: "Yeah that's how I feel but I have a few issues with my ex and his lack of sexual prowess. He really wasn't that good in bed so it led to a lot of fights I just need a guy who is sexually compatible and confident in himself. Yeah, he didn't ever like, take me out. Ya know.

Him: Well I...

Her: Yeah it was just kinda weird, he was cheap too, never wanted to take me anywhere nice or spoil me just the same places every weekend. It's like I don't want to be bored with the same things all the time...

So she proceeded to continue for about 5 minutes as to why this guy sucked so bad. Suffice to say he didn't call her back. She put all her cards on the table and not the good ones. I'm sure she's a lovely person but the person he spoke to came across as vapid and not very considerate. It's not attractive to anyone when someone just vomits an abundance of information you didn't ask for, especially when it's trashing someone else. Just remember it is the first date and just only that for now. Leave your baggage and drama at the door, you want to just focus on seeing if there's an ember of similarities and at least strong mutual interests.

Now if you're a person who just can't keep it all in. There are ways you can tell them your life story with patience and a sprinkle of panache. Just give it time and make it more about your date.

The idea is that you don't spend the first couple of minutes talking about how this is one of the hottest summers ever and more wack small talk. But you want to reveal the right amount of information.

To be frank, the first date isn't for you to use someone as a sounding board. Now don't go all Jason Bourne on them and hardly tell them a shred of information but just be subtle and cool.

Think:

"It didn't end in the best way with my last boyfriend"

Vs.

"Yeah my asshole ex burned my stuff all over our front lawn, then he hacked into my facebook account and sent nudes to my friends and family, what a jerk right"

Yeah, one of those stories I just mentioned is based on something that actually happened and that was the abbreviated version!

Look, you can be honest, that's one of the main themes of this book. But you can also be honest without having to spout out the most awkward and revealing pieces of information. There is a time and a place and it sure as hell isn't the first date. When you are honest with your own truths and vulnerability there's a difference between that and just sitting there and having a moan fest. No one wants to hear it. Go tell it to yo momma. Cause the rest of us ain't got time.

I'll never forget this date I had. It was terrible. The worst thing about it was this, it started off great. I swear to god. We had a great conversation about our favorite comedy tv shows and promptly reenacted some key scenes from Brooklyn 99. Let me tell you when the date went south. Sooooo south. She proceeded to tell me about her car accident.

"Trey you heartless bastard!"

Yeah, I know right, how can I be abhorred by someone's car accident details. That wasn't even the bad part. It was the fact she proceeded to go into rich detail about the car accident and how she lost her leg. She then began to complain about how men get turned off when they have sex with her because she has a wooden leg. She mentioned that it's hard to find a guy who was attracted to her sexually when she reveals the wooden leg. Trust me, she went on for at least 15 minutes. I was shocked. But I didn't want to be a prick and interrupt so I listened on.

Just when I thought it was over, she said this…

"Wanna see it?"

I froze. What should I do? On one hand, if I say no. I could end up making her feel shitty and just magnify her already glowing insecurities with it. On the other hand, if I say yes, maybe I could make her feel a little better and alleviate some anxieties she might have. But wait, how have we even gotten this far in the conversation? Why does she think it's okay to prattle on about this for so long!

Guess what I went with.

"I'd love to see your leg".

In the middle of a pretty swanky wine bar, at full capacity, I might add. She proceeds to pull up the left side of her dress, pull down her left tights to reveal this pretty cool-looking mahogany leg. It actually wasn't nearly as bad as she made out. It was just the over-long story and TMI that came before and the fact that she had no filter. Ya see being genuine and authentic on a date and having zero filters are not one in the same thing. There are times when you can talk for 30 minutes straight on a date. But not usually the first date. You see the person who's hearing these 15 -30 minute stories doesn't know you well or long enough to care. Enough rapport and trust just hasn't settled in to go into such great detail. The person isn't nearly as emotionally invested, yet. Those things can always be discussed but you have to decide how much connection has been built up enough for you to be so raw so fast. Deeply rooted personal conversations can only be inserted via the consequence of time and trust. It's you who has to decipher when that's there.

There was nothing wrong with what she said, it was all just kinda weird.

You see, no one cares or gives a crap about how mean your boss is on the first date. Or how much you hate your landlord. At least not yet, save it. There's a time and place to vent about life, it's just not the first date. Please take my kindly given advice on this one. After all, you've already paid for it.

Still, need some clear-cut things you shouldn't say on a first date? I'll help you out.

    A.   You're way cuter/hotter/attractive than me:

A thousand no's. What!? Why would you even say that? That immediately kills any kind of value you have with this person and they'll assume you're just kind of insecure. When have you ever had a discussion with your friends and said, "Hey, you know what, I am dying to date someone really insecure". Exactly! you never have. No one wants that. Even if you're thinking it, don't say it out loud. Besides, your parents love you and think you're great. So just chill out.

B. Sorry I usually don't tell people what area I live in:

This is one that irks me a little. You're more than willing to meet someone in a public place but won't tell them where you're based? Furthermore, in the back of your mind, you still think this person might cut you into little pieces yet you entertained the notion of a date!? Usually when I say, "Cool what area do you live in?". When the person isn't comfortable telling me I think to myself, that's a little odd. What could possibly happen? Am I going to travel to your neighborhood and knock on 20,000 doors searching for your unrequited love? Am I going to stalk your life and make it my life's goal to find out where you live? No, in fact, I don't even think real-life stalkers have enough time for that shit. This only happens in the movies. Relax, if you tell someone what area you're based in they're not going to be walking around there all day hoping to bump into you. Stop watching CSI and Dateline and any kind of murder podcast it'll rot your brain and make you paranoid about dating. This could happen, but the chances are very slim to none.

When you say something like that it puts up defenses and guards where there doesn't need to be. It ends up making the person feel like an idiot for even asking. When you refuse to disclose that information what it says to the other person is. They think I'm trying to find their address, they think I have ulterior motives and they don't even trust me enough to even tell me the general area. Hell, I've told people at the bus stop the area I live in.

Me "I live in Brooklyn"

Person @ the bus stop: (Now I can stalk his life. I don't know where he lives exactly but if I knock on enough doors I can find him)

Ya see!? This stuff doesn't happen IRL.

C. You're too hot to be single:

Urgh, gag! I know, I know. You think you're Don Juan spouting outlines like that. But that right there is exactly why it doesn't work. It's a line. Women and men can see it 100 miles out, it's corny, cliched, and needy. What you're demonstrating are a few low-value things. One, you base singleness only on physical appearance alone. I.E you failed to factor in that despite how attractive this individual is, they just might have an atrocious personality, or the last relationship they had just didn't work out. Two, you have already put this person in "object" status just by a comment like that and now you are nothing more than a bison running along with the other herd. Don't say it, it's very weak and requires not that many brain cells for such a sentence to be released from that overhanging caping chasm of yours. You're better than this.

D. You'd need to drink way more alcohol if you want to hang with me.

You damn alcoholic, choose another hobby.

E. So did you enjoy the date?

No one really likes being put on the spot, especially at the end of a date, good or bad. Just chill and be a little patient before you ask that question. If you're consistent and moderately persistent with your pursuit of courtship then you'll meet the right person and you'll never have to ask that question. If you feel like you do have to ask, I'd consider asking yourself how interested they really are? You can ask, just not right at the end of the date. I would encourage you to vocalize it yourself. But do not put that person on the spot like that. Because in most cases if they didn't. I don't know a single person that would respond, "To be honest it was kinda crap, would have rather watched American Idol".

(Who am I kidding, no one watches American Idol)

F. Not to be racist but/Not to sound sexist/Not to be homophobic, can I play devil's advocate…

Eeesh. Avoid all of those, if you can at least on the first date (Or ever). The first date isn't really the place to get heavy into political, socio-economic, racial, and battle of the sexes talks. I mean you can if you want to and it's not completely forbidden by any social normality but it's risky. Imagine it like this. You drive home sober after hitting the bars, the risk is very low. You drive home 4 shots and 5 beers in, the risk is pretty high. So you can totally do it but you might die, get pulled over, kill someone else, damage your car, and so forth. Metaphorically speaking, a car wreck on a first date is uninsurable. Avoid those topics if you can. Also don't be racist, sexist, or homophobic. Spread the love man!

G. "To be honest, I don't think OJ did it"

So gross. That person will run away from you so fast your head will spin.

H. How many people have you slept with?

I'm sad that I even have to type this up. But don't ask for someone's "body count". It's kinda gross and it just paints you out to be nosey, needy, and a rather desperate individual. As if by some way the lesser the body count the purer that person is!? I don't think so. It's one of those things that I'm sure you'll always be curious about. But in my experience when anyone's ever told me, say we've been dating for a few months. The conversation never ended well. Avoid it. Don't talk about it and if they ask yours. Just be polite, "I'd rather not talk about that on the first date if that's okay". It's just all a bit weird and intrusive if someone asks that. So just put yourself out of that equation by not asking it.

I. I'm just looking to meet new people, nothing serious:

This is probably one of the most transparent overused and insincere phrases I've heard and read time and time again. That phrase is about as real as a reality TV production.

Gimme a break. Really? People like this make me laugh. If you are looking to meet new people and not looking for anything serious join Facebook join a few MeetUp groups. That's like me logging into PornHub and saying. I'm actually not on here for porn, I'm trying to figure out if this Mailman is actually going to make his deliveries on time. Oh shit, that's bad. I mean "I'm here to see if the plumber actually fixes the toilet". Ya see that it just doesn't work right!? Just own it. If you're looking to date around and hopefully find someone that sticks, be honest. If you were truly just looking to meet "new people" you'd never accept someone wasting your time just to be "friends", especially of the opposite sex. Deep down in that lovely heart of yours, there is a glimmer of hope for romance the tiniest flame that something might happen! You know there is.

Be honest with yourself and them. They'll admire you and be attracted to you for it. Forget all this, I'm trying to play it cool bullshit because people see right through it. They're too polite to call you out on your insincerity to call a duck a duck. I'm telling you right now, if you own up to what you're looking for, guess what. Eventually, you'll get ... WHAT YOU'RE LOOKING FOR. The universe has a way of giving you what you vocalize far more than any internalization. If you own what you truly want it's also a way to weed out the people who just are not on the same page. If someone isn't looking for the same things as you are. This is an easy process of elimination.

16. The Risky Conversations…

"Turn a perceived risk into an asset." – **Aaron Patzer**

This is all up to the connection, remember this whole book is about going outside some of the social norms and just being the best version of yourself, so if topics of taboo come up. Taboos such as sex, religion, politics, and all that good stuff. Just imagine things you wouldn't say at work and if it comes up you can absolutely discuss it, but proceed with caution. Emphasis on the "if it comes up" If anything you want to avoid any similarities you would have with a discussion at work right?

> For example what if after 4 dates you realize this person is a religious zealot who thinks everyone is gonna burn in hell, for letting gay people live their lives and be happy. Or an overly enthusiastic gun nut who wants his 5-year-old kids to learn how to shoot guns. It's up to you but it's a murky area trust me. I'd air on the side of caution but if you really want to know, if this is your absolute deal-breaker if you can't possibly go on another date until you know. Go ahead and ask. Religion is a huge deal-breaker for some people and it may be the difference be-

tween dating and a full-blown relationship. There are smooth ways you can do this, don't hug as soon as you meet, grab a seat and say, "So who do you worship?". Of course, that's not going to happen. But like I said if it naturally occurs and is brought up in a manner that isn't intrusive, aggressive, and a pleasant point of the conversation. In an alternative way, when they mention Xmas or something. You can say something like, "So are you quite religious?" See the difference there from the previous question about religion.

Occasionally it's difficult to really make sure the conversation is perfectly appropriate and that you are ever so polite and say all the right things. I say screw that. Just say what comes naturally to you and if the person doesn't like it, then that's not the type of personality you are best suited with. I really mean it. Do you want to have conversations with people where you always feel like you have to censor yourself? That sounds lame. But remember what I said in the previous chapter. This is a gentle balance and it's up to you to master it.

Whatever you do, do not I repeat do not rehearse your conversation pieces in the mirror. You'll end up with an egg on your lovely face. I remember reading a study published in Personality and Individual Differences from sciencedirect.com. In the study, they found pre-planned lines and badly prepared dad jokes suck. People are not stupid, they can read right past all that nonsense. So for the last time don't do it. Have a conversation about most things that people do, you know things like, exercise, movies, music, books, tv shows, what's happening in the news, the current socio-economic climate, how much pizza can you eat in one sitting? But just speak about common topics. Who do you know out there that doesn't like music!? Or tv or movies. I always use those as a go-to. I guarantee you you'll have at least one movie or song in common and you can totally vibe off that. If you don't then you'll have a new movie or song to listen to and that's a great conversation piece if there's another date. Most human beings have a basic understanding of crossing the conversational line with people and I'm sure you're one of them. But just in case let me give you some differences so you can be real, speak about things freely, and not offend the other person. This way you'll have a great dynamic conversation the two of you will never forget.

The Vs Scale:

- "I'm not remotely religious anyone who is, I lose respect for them" **Vs** "Yeah, I've never really been too religious"
- "Yeah, f**k the current US president" **Vs**. "I hope he does a good job but he's not the guy/woman for me"
- "Kids? can't stand 'em they cost too much and they stink" **Vs**. "I'm not sure how I feel about them, guess I'll cross that road when I come to it"
- "Yeah, I love me some good ass sex, nice and sweaty, balls deep baby! yeaaahhhh" **Vs**. "I appreciate great sex with someone who I really care about and could see a future with"

Remember you don't and shouldn't follow these to the law. But this just gives you a good idea of how to talk about slightly taboo subjects with ease and class. After all, you want your date to leave with a mindset of wow. Seriously just wow.

You know the question I hate the most, "So uh, what do you do for a living" God, please give me a break. Everyone asks that question, I get it. It's going to come up but save it near the end of the date or even the second or allow it to come up from them. It's just so overdone. I would go for the heart. By that I mean figure out what really makes this person tick, get to the emotions and the passions as previously referenced. "What kind of things do you adore in a relationship". Really get to some moderately meaty subjects. I read an article by Dan Ariely he poses the notion that you should be asking more questions that are kinda personal. Yeah I know, it's kinda risky but why not? People didn't get far in life by playing things so close to the belt. Something like, "How many dates have you been on this month". I think it's a fair question. If they're not open to answering, just move the subject over. Look, you're trying to find someone special. Let's not play games here and tiptoe around subjects. Let's have a raw, enigmatic, and inquisitive conversation. Let's flesh out who you both really are and leave the date thinking....Holy shit I've never had a first date where I had to be so self-reflective and yet have a fun conversation all at the same time. Set the stage of brilliance. Be the person that they want to see again and again. A polarizing and captivating personality is one that doesn't play by the rules but has respect enough to simmer around the fundamentals of the rules. Not by corny lines or tricky date tactics but just by being you. Because guess what, you really are awesome. I guarantee you there are a lot of people that deeply love and care about you because you're generally a great person. You can increase that awesomeness by expanding upon hidden internal attributes you may not even have known you had.

I would actually go as far as to have some fun with it, maybe play a game. If you ask each other a set of questions and if the other person is uncomfortable with it, they can say "Veto". That way you can move along quickly without any awkwardness and have some fun. Either way, you're both the masters of your own ship and can guide the conversation any way you want. But whatever you do, make sure the conversation isn't too run of the mill. Of course nothing wrong with a perfectly good small talk first date scenario. But the idea of that makes me want to throw up inside my mouth. I'm also not sure of many people who would want to stretch an elevator-type conversation to more than 10 minutes.

It's the right amount of information that you choose to divulge. Men and women value someone who is vulnerable and you should definitely release some personal details about who you are and what you really stand for. But there is a stark difference to this:

You: "Yeah, my asshole ex didn't even return my stuff, what a terrible person right?! He had cat shit in his apartment and his feet smell like moldy cheese. Gross as hell right!? It was like I couldn't even get a word in with him, what a prick!"

VS:

You: "Yeah I got out of a pretty bad relationship about 6 months ago. For few months I was really hurting. But I moved on".

You really need to give this person a sense of who you are. So allowing them to see an honest version of yourself whilst also revealing some home truths could give them a real side of you. Vulnerability is very hard not to be warmed up to. I'm not saying you should use it as a tool to get people to fall for you. But it should be classed as a tool to allow you to be stronger with who you are. Thus giving you the strength to be more vocal with your truths. Learning to reveal your own personal truths gives you such a higher degree of blossoming confidence it won't be long till that affects more than your dating life.

I find it helpful to look at the date like catching up with an old friend I haven't seen in a while. Only you're trying to see what things have changed with them and fleshing them out a little. For example something I like to say after the obligatory welcoming is.

"How have things been this week?"

It's simple but it's effective. I try and speak and communicate with the person as if we've done so before. This allows me to be completely open with who I am and leaves no room for "faking it". One thing I find really funny is when I'm at a coffee shop and you can tell two people are on an awkward first date. It makes me laugh inside my head all the time. I give myself a gentle reminder that I don't ever want that to be me. So be sincere with yourself and speak to them as if you are familiar acquaintances. If you put that mindset firmly in your head you'll allow your date to feel very comfortable and the conversation will just flow.

When you're trying to be open and forthright you open the floor for the other person to meet you in the middle and open up as well. That's when you both start to enjoy transparent and candid communication. Then it begins reaching that peak of an enjoyable romantic connection. Those stimulating and emotional points begin as a light flame, it's up to you to fan it into a roaring fire.

Have you ever heard of something called Negative Reflection? It's interesting as it's a small facet of vulnerability. Essentially what you're doing is exposing a minor weakness in yourself. For example:

Me: "I'm not the best at small talk. Sometimes if I see a work colleague at the grocery store, it will be a quick conversation with a very awkward goodbye".

Her: Me too! I totally suck at elevator conversations!

You see how that works. It's a small thing to do on dates but goes back to really talking about what the hell you want and being frank with each other about who you both are.

I have far more respect for someone who's able to open up just a little about some of their vulnerabilities and weaknesses on a first date. It makes me a little weak at the knees and I admire that person. Who doesn't appreciate that right?

Remember you want to have a great charming conversation but you want to flesh this person out and really figure out what they want from their relationship future and who they are as a person. Any person you meet has so much more depth than an attractive face. The key is to avoid the same old business mixer small talk. It's just kinda boring and I have a feeling the reason you picked this book is that you are not boring, you want to expand on what you know is in your emotional basement.

17. I'll Get The Check (Who Pays!?)

"A man is only loved under the condition that he provide something" - **Chris Rock**

In the last 100 years, society has made a slow but steady change with gender roles, who does what around the house and how you raise a family in a two-parent household, who's bringing in the bacon. Yet despite this, you know the one thing that hasn't really changed that much? Who pays for the date!

If you don't believe me, just scroll on your Instagram, follow a few meme or quote accounts and count the huge number of memes trolling so-called "cheapskates" and various people screenshotting messages shaming those men out there who have failed to do "what's expected" by way of paying for dates.

Paying for dates is rarely what's discussed. If it is, it's usually between the same sex as they rant about the fact they have to pay or the fact that he didn't. That's really always going to be the defining moment with dating in this new world we live in. **What's expected vs what's discussed**. The reason why so many first dates fail is that more often or not it's what's expected that frustrates one or both parties. When something is expected and it doesn't come to fruition on the first date the person often leaves annoyed and will proceed to call their friend and rant or complain on TikTok, Facebook or post some passive-aggressive subliminal Instagram that no one gets or cares about. Something that could have been so wonderful has ended up being another story biting the dust just because of small inflated expectations.

The notion of who should pay, a man or a woman comes across as very heteronormative, usually, it comes down to the man and in some cases, there are some men who find this to be a bit of financial hindrance, imagine if you're a bloke and you make 40,000 a year before tax and someone you barely know expects a nice expensive date. For some gentlemen who choose to foot the bill, there are cases where they can't help but feel a little used. Before you throw your hands in the air with quick offense and rage. Not to worry, I'm fully aware of the degree of male privilege to which I have, women don't have it remotely easy in the dating world either and I promise I'm not trying to paint the man as a victim. But for now, we're talking about who pays. I also am fully aware that if a girl pays some men might feel "emasculated" (BS by the way) or he might think he's "getting some". Fair play it's not easy for either sex.

I'm with you both, promise.

So allow me to digest some ways we can break through those minor issues and have you enjoy the company of the date without feeling like your bank account just got shot in the belly.

In the last 10 years dating has changed in the biggest way possible.

And it's all because of our great strides in technology. It's changed the dating game so much to a point where it's barely recognizable.

The argument is always this. The person who asks the person out on the first date pays. Which is a little bit sneaky. How many women do you know out there who have taken the initiative and asked the man out for the first date and paid? Not a lot, in my experience, even when a lady has asked me out I've still been expected to pay to some degree, so I figured that rule is more of a smokescreen or debris we're still trying to clean up from the last 50 years of dating. You men out there better get ready to empty those wallets. I'm sure there's a decent majority of strong independent women who have paid a few times on a first date. For that, I applaud and encourage you to hold true to what makes you comfortable. The truth of the matter is 8/10 men will always be expected to pay.

Not the worst thing in the world, especially if the date turns out to be incredible. But in this socio-political climate we're living in these days we're all about equality for women and men. I'm so for it! But it doesn't really translate over in the dating world. Even the most ardent women I've dated who are feminists like for men to pay for the first date, they want chivalry to be alive and well. Also, your pockets to be just as lively.

So, men, you're going to have to exercise your financial demons and pull out that wallet. As for women, I can only speak for myself. But even though I have every intention of paying for the first date. Nothing warms my heart more when a woman offers to pay and is sincere about it. Of course, I won't let her because I'd like to bring in a bit of cliched chivalry, but it's still a sweet notion nonetheless. From all the gentlemen in my friendship circle, they like it when a woman offers too.

On the other hand, the fake reach is a load of rubbish and men can see it from a mile off. Genuinely ask, "Can I help?". If you really want to impress him. Sincerely offer to pay. If he gets the wrong idea and assumes he's going to get something out of this he's not the guy. As a man, I think it's very telling when a woman offers to pay. A few times when the ladies offered I decided to roll the dice and let them. What I always found was the women who were no longer interested cause I let them pay vs the women who I ended up seeing again said a lot about their personality. If people get bent out of shape based on societal norms maybe that's not for you or maybe it is. But if someone offers to pay and has no intention of doing so, what does that say about them?

I did something crazy last Saturday night. When I was out with some friends I walked down a busy downtown area full of bars and clubs and asked **30 women**, should a man pay for the first couple of dates? It started as I was in a heated debate with some friends male and female, there were about 8 of us. 5 girls and 3 men. I said, "I don't mind paying for the first few dates but then after that, it would be nice if the lady I was dating, paid a bit". I got verbally eviscerated. The constant argument from them is that a true gentleman always pays. One of the women proudly exclaimed that when she dated the last boyfriend she had. She never paid for one date. They dated for a year. She didn't pay for one date! For a year! WTF. No wonder she stayed with him, hell I'd date him for free dates for the rest of the year! Cor blimey!

- I walked down Main street and asked 30 different women or groups of girls what they thought. Granted this isn't the fairest test, but I needed something.

Can you guess what the response was?

- 22 of them said yes he should, it's the gentlemanly thing to do. The irony of this is that most of them came across as headstrong, intelligent, professional women. So why would they not want to contribute in the initial stages?

- What does the modern woman look like for you today? I think of women like Beyonce, Jennifer Lawrence, Ellen Degeneres, Michelle Obama, Tina Fey, Kim Scott, Oprah Winfrey, and some other brilliant women of today.

Stars like Beyonce have empowered women further, and rightly so, she's taught them to be independent (Independent Woman) to be a survivor, and to tell that boy BYE!! I can't tell you the number of times I've heard that phrase uttered by my female friends. Today's independent woman is just that, independent, successful, confident, and a goddess. But why does this independence come at a shocking stop when it comes to the initial stages of dating. Why are principles of reciprocity thrown out the window?

Before you start telling yourself I'm not a gentleman and I'm a cheapskate. Let me explain my rule of thumb. When I ask a woman on a date I expect to pay. After all, I asked right? The next two dates I plan to pay too. But after the third date, I have to positively assume the woman in question is interested in me or she wouldn't entertain any kind of date. I don't do this because I enjoy spending money on women I may or may not see again. I do this because it's expected of me. So why would she not at least consider going dutch, or plan and pay for the date? I'm not saying I stop seeing the women after that. But my attraction dwindles ever so slightly. I'd like to be with a long-term partner who values reciprocity and wants to be a team.

So this whole independence ideology comes across as limited and slightly selective, at least that's how it seems. So I started thinking about this all week. On Wednesday I attended a young professional's mixer. I let people know I'm writing a book and ask them the following question.

"At what point should dating be equal? Especially with who pays and stuff"

The men responded with:

"Man I got a mortgage and an HOA to pay, we split right down the middle"

"I say give it about 3 months a woman can start paying, but I don't really care to be honest"

"Haha women do the fake reach of the purse, but they don't wanna pay, I hate that shit man"

"After the first date if she doesn't offer I can find someone else. I'm liquid"

"This is what annoys me dude, it's like they say they want equal stuff. But the moment they have to pay their way, they call us cheap and refuse another date"

"If the lady insists after I offer I'll let her pay"

"I'm a man, I'll always take care of my woman. A real man takes care of the person he's with, she don't gotta worry bout nothin' with me"

"If I take a lady out bowling, then dinner and then we go to the movies after and she says I'll pay for that. I'll try and bag her for sure, that's a keeper man"

"The man always pays, that's just how I've been raised"

"It's difficult because I feel like women want a free meal or want to be treated like princesses, I'm looking for my woman I'm not just trying to feed her"

"I'm asking for the date I pay, but I won't be buying a 3-course meal for one date. If she invites me out, she's paying, that's it, I'm not trying to get finessed".

"A guy pays, that's just how it is, right?"

"I think it just depends who I date"

Interestingly enough, if not very predictable save one or two comments. So I approached a few different groups of women.

The women said

"I might consider offering to pay, but if he lets me, I'm totally ignoring his text after"

"If we go to coffee or something and he doesn't pay, he's a cheapskate, that man can not raise a family"

"I never really expect to pay, if he's a gentleman he'll always pay"

"The man should always pay for the first couple of dates, show me I'm worth it"

"Women should never invite men on a date, god I can't believe this is how dating is these days"

"If I'm being invited I'm never gon pay, but if he wants to lock me down I'll consider paying my way"

"I always bring my purse just in case, but I expect the man to pay"

"If he doesn't pay, it's not a date and he's nothing but a friend"

"To prove I'm not that type of girl, I'll pay for a drink here or there. A whole date, though…? Is we in a relationship?"

"I disagree with all these women, we're supposed to be empowered yet we don't wanna pay? If I'm interested after the first date, I'll pay. Also really like planning dates too"

"This isn't the 1900s I have no problem paying"

"I don't need to be looked after, I'll go dutch I just don't want him thinking I'll sleep with him".

"Look at Michelle Obama; she was well off before she met Barack, so yeah."

I say this, always offer. Man or woman and you can figure it out amongst yourselves. But for the most part, if I haven't already said it, men. You'll always be expected to pay for the first date so get creative and woo your date.

However, if you're reading and you'll still a little confused you can have some fun with this and not have to be so rigid. I'll give you some extended ideas.

Just split the bill

Ooh. This one takes balls of steel because some men and women are very specific about this and you might very well rub them the wrong way. For some people, the use of financial expenditure is a good judgment of how into them the other person is. So when you ask to split they may think you're not into them. Yeah, it's not the most romantic so I would do that if you don't feel too much of a connection. If you're interested are you really gonna sit there and take that person's hard-earned cash.

What do you do?

If they tell you they're in school but you on the other hand have a 6 figure job. You might want to be a little considerate and pay.

None of you even have to pay -

Let's say if you just couldn't possibly be taken away from your hard-earned cash. Go somewhere for free, the park, the beach, a gallery, the museum, the library, a little picnic there's so many free events around your local city you just have to know where to look!!

18. Don't Lead People On! (Rejection)

"The biggest coward of a man is to awaken the love of a woman without the intention of loving her." - **Bob Marley**

One of the most frustrating things that were constantly echoed to me throughout all the focus groups I conducted, was about this...

The texts/call after.

You get both parties who are trying to play it cool so the texts start gradually getting duller and both of them quit. Or both sexes wait for the other person to text first and they both end up not hearing from the person. EVEN IF THEY'RE BOTH INTERESTED. What the hell kind of human sense does that even make!? But this happens time and time again and a lot of people are not willing to overcome their pride and get over it.

Guess what either way you win, if you only but communicate.

If you communicate and say, "Hey had a great time, let's do it again". If they don't respond, that makes them emotionally stunted and not adult enough to say they're not interested. You dodged a bullet. Move on, remember it's far more of a reflection of them. If they do respond and say, "I'm sorry I'm just not interested". You have closure, move on. They gave you the respect you deserve by taking an hour out of your day to see them. Or they could respond and say, "I'd love too!" Either Way, you WIN!! Yes. You read this correctly. All you have to do is put yourself out there, again and again, success, love, victory, and happiness never came to a single person who didn't take a risk. No, let me correct that riskS. You're going to have to go through a lot of rejections before you even get close to what you truly want. High-risk high reward. Go for it and tell them how you feel even if it's a simple one-sentence text.

The lines of interest are so blurred these days.

For men and women. If you're a man you don't want to be too forward and go in for a kiss especially if you are not certain of her interest level. You might be kissing someone without consent! But if she's interested then it shouldn't be an issue so there is that fine line. If you are a woman just cause you're interested doesn't mean you're ready for a first kiss or not, so it's a very, very fine line. That's why you have to let them know! If you want that first kiss, be honest. "I actually kinda like you". Boom they know you're interested, just like that. Now nobody is confused and if it's not reciprocated then so be it. Who cares. There are also indirect signals. There are some classics, direct eye contact, laughing at their jokes, and giving them a subtle touch on the arm or hands, that long gaze. These are clear world-renowned signs of attraction it's letting you know where their feelings lie.

Be very careful with that glowing ego of yours. Chill, it's okay everybody has one but you have to be careful in your assumptions. For example, about 3 years ago I went on a date with a lovely lady. She was nice enough, but from my viewpoint, she didn't have much about her apart from prattling on about CrossFit. For 30 minutes, bloody hell! 30 minutes. Long story short I wasn't interested. As soon as the date ended I got home and felt like the gentlemanly thing would be to tell her I'm not interested. I sent her this:

Me: "Hey Sarah, thanks for taking the time to come and meet me tonight. I didn't really feel a connection tonight, so let's be friends"

Her: "Yeah, no offense I wasn't interested either"

Me: "Well great, no harm no foul. Have a nice evening"

Her :

I offended her so much she didn't even wish me luck either. Yikes. The key thing here is don't be cocky enough to assume that even though you're not interested, they're interested. They might not be either. Yes, I get it, perhaps in your world almost everyone you meet fancies the pants of you. But not everyone. So if you want to, you could let them know how you feel after the date. But in some cases, it's just not that deep. Letting someone know you're not interested is a skill in itself. You have to do it in a way that's not assumptive, but at the same time not leading someone on. It really is a tightrope of emotions. But you can learn to easily walk it. Just don't prolong what you know is going to happen out of sheer fear for the results and hurting someone's feelings. You're better than that.

If the shoe was on the other foot. How would you feel?

What you can do in this scenario in order to not come across as brutal or heartless is wait to see how interested the other party really is. For women in this case you might have it a little easier. Social dating norms dictate that men should lead from the beginning of the first date till the end. So for the most part if the man's really interested he'll ask for a 2nd date. Not in all cases but for the most part. That's when you can politely turn him down. Now granted, as I mentioned earlier if it's a first date you really owe no explanation and you can just vanish, I don't recommend it. But it is an option. However, if a man has taken the time to plan, pay for, and prepare the date. I would at least let them know you're not interested. You don't even owe them an explanation but just let them know that it's a no for you if they ask for the 2nd date. That's the best and most respectful thing you can do. Not all people can handle rejection well but if you develop a habit of being truthful and respectful to someone's feelings it will help your growth as a lovely human being. Remember we're trying to fix dating. That doesn't just include fixing it for you. But maybe it involves fixing it for other people too. Maybe that person who might often get ghosted appreciates you being honest and given that small glimmer of hope from someone else. All because you were honest.

For guys, you're in tricky territory. Because it really depends on the girl in question. As always I'm not going to put all of you lovely women out there into one basket. As I said, it's subtly expected that the man will continue to pursue and ask for a 2nd date if they're interested. Even if the woman in question is very much interested, she will seldom be direct and say how much she likes you and push for a 2nd date, it happens for sure. It's just not a regular occurrence. Some women will continue texting to show interest and drop subtle hints that they'd like to go on a 2nd date. But like I said though, it's in your hands to get it going. Trust me I get your frustrations and their slight paradoxical nature. It's kinda funny actually. Cause if a woman is interested, she'll wait for you to make the first move for a 2nd date so she can embrace her femininity and be pursued. If she's not interested she'd be happy to never hear from you again. So either way, in most cases you must bite the bullet and be a little direct or you'll never really know where the interest level is. It's quite simple, don't play games, don't try and be "low key". Just be clear with your intentions. We're not about wasting time in this book. We're about being direct. If you don't manifest what you want, you'll never be in a good position to get it.

The craziest thing about this notion is even when you're direct and honest with someone and ask for that same courtesy sometimes they can't even meet you in the middle. Check out this text thread I received from my buddy Terrell:

Terrell: Hey! I had a great time tonight, hope you had a great time too!

Her: I did, thanks for the tacos!

Terrell: We should go out sometime next week if you're interested?

Her: Yeah, maybe.

Terrell: Haha if not. That's okay but I enjoyed getting to know you. Would like to see you again.

Her: I'm not sure, to be honest

Terrell: Okay, well let me know.

The poor guy, he was pretty direct and she refused to even give him a smidgen of clear cut, yes or no. How would you feel if you were just trying to figure out where you stand and you couldn't get a straight answer from anyone? It would be so frustrating!

Check out this text thread:

Rob: Yo guys you all still down to hit up the driving range today?

Jack: Yeah I might come through

Carlos: Yeah just let me know I should be there

Ted: I'll let you know gotta run some errands.

Are any of these solid plans? Would you bet all your Saturday plans on this?!

Ladies and gents, please. Do the right thing and be real with where you're at. If you are uncomfortable with being forthcoming, sure you can ghost. But if they flat out ask you what the deal is. You gotta respond. I mean in most cases this is via text. You don't even have to deal with the awkwardness of audibly speaking on the phone. So do the right thing for god's sake. Be a good human. This type of "real-time" feedback when you date will work wonders and good or bad they'll really appreciate it. The wonders your good karma will go through will be brilliant.

Here's a quick hypothetical for you -

You: "I had a great time, tonight. I'd like to see you again"

Response 1: "I'd like that a lot"

Response 2: "I think it would be best if we stayed friends"

Response 3:

Response 4: "Yeah, maybe"

Ya, see how simple that is!? You can really only get 3 answers or a variation of those 3.

1. They're interested
2. They're not interested
3. They're happy just to ignore you.
4. They're indecisively indifferent

Either way, you get the answers you need. Don't be afraid of rejection. They won't be the first and they won't be the last to reject you, so move past that and remember it's all part of the process of attraction and finding out what you like and don't like. Most importantly find out who you really are. But I always say, just let the person know. If you don't it's a little hurtful and not nice. There are some people who it might hurt a little then after a few hours they'll be over it. Or a day or two and they'll be like, meh. But then there are those poor folks who take it very personally and would think about it all week. Don't be that person who has that kind of effect on anyone. Just let them know. Be a part of the solution and not the problem, make that person believe in the goodness of dating even if it doesn't work out.

We've tarnished dating a little too much. Yes, I know what your thinking, "Another piece saying millenials have ruined yet another thing". Fine, maybe it isn't on us to shoulder the whole responsibility of changing the dating scape. But we were the generation at the forefront of using the technology to date to our advantage more than any other generation before us. We're the beta generation of the online dating world. We are the ones that made online dating a commonplace and not some creepy man child living in his mum's basement. It's time for us to make a change. It all starts with you.

I understand though. Sometimes you may feel like the date was a terrible time and you wish you never wasted that hour. Take into consideration that poor sap on the other side that could be calling their mum up as soon as they get home and proclaiming how this might be the one! You could be laughing in your head as you drive home, whilst the other person has already picked out the wedding ring.

Us westerners are the masters of pretending just to be polite and not hurt someone's feelings. So even if you feel like the date was terrible. I'm sure you were pleasant and not an asshole about it. So the other person might not know. So like I said, let them know, good or bad. But either way, one of you has to express interest in seeing each other again if there is interest. Or there's a strong chance you'll never have an understanding of what even happened. Don't allow it to chance, take control of the situation as much as you can, and be genuine. That way you'll know. Or you will clearly communicate with the other person where you're at.

Still, struggling to see an opportunity for change? Let me help you with some clever rejection texts and "I'm interested' texts (You know you're not gonna call them)

Brutal Texts (Only send these where they're complete and utter wankers) -

    A.   Yeah I'm not really feeling it

    B.   Sorry, not interested

    C.   No way!

    D.   You lied about your profile picture

    E.   I don't want to body shame, but you're not my type

    F.   You voted for ……… that's just too much for me

    G.   I don't even think you wash your ass, issa no for me dawg

Polite

    A.   You seem cool AF but let's be friends

    B.   It was a lot of fun, loved getting to know you. You're going to meet someone great

    C.   I didn't feel like we had similar interests but thanks so much for the meal

    D.   You have the right to be with someone who matches your personality perfectly

    E.   I'm not in the best place to date right now, but thanks for your time

Serious

A. I don't see this going anywhere relationship-wise

B. I don't really see a future with you

C. I'm looking for someone who can guide me and lead me spiritually in the eyes of the lord

D. I need someone who is financially stable, has a good credit score, and isn't currently in school, I really appreciate the coffee though

E. Your medical impairments are something I don't think I can take on right now

F. I don't usually date .... person

For the love of God, please avoid statements like, "Good luck out there" or "happy hunting" and "best of luck". It comes across as a little condescending with sprinkles of arrogance. Just avoid it. Could you imagine going for a job interview and after a few days they call you up to tell you that you didn't get the job? Then they say, "but good luck out there". You'll be thinking. "Man, kiss my arse, I wanted the job. Don't wish me luck, give me the job" . Have you ever received a rejection email after the job you wanted turned you down? How do you feel when they say, "Best of luck on your future endeavors". Your not sitting there thinking, "oh me oh my I sure hope I have good luck too". No, your pissed! You wanted the job, damn it! So that just comes across as them coming from a higher pedestal. "You were good but not good enough". Now of course we know that's not really what it means, maybe you just didn't have enough qualifications, experience, or even a good culture add. There are logical pragmatic reasons as to why it just won't work out. But when someone gets rejected they're not thinking straight, logically, or pragmatically. They think, "I am a good match, you're wrong. Kiss my ass!".

But remember this, after you've had time to process getting rejected or being the rejector. It's going to happen far more than you'd like. There are very few people who have a constant "winning" streak when it comes to dating and if they do, it's bound to happen eventually. For those people, it will be far worse than those of us who have suffered our fair share of rejection. So welcome it with open arms the same way a teenager welcomes a 12 pack of Mountain Dew. It will build character and make you far more mature and ready to handle when this situation will inevitably occur at some point. And trust me, it will happen. A lot of people spend their lives wanting to avoid rejection and failure. But dating is one of those places where rejection and failure are the easiest, less impactful, and the least life-altering.

Think about it right now with me, would you rather:

Get rejected for a job Vs Get rejected on a meaningless first date?

Fail on a big work project Vs. Fail on a first date?

Get rejected for an art festival application Vs. Rejected by someone you barely know

Fail at your first 7-mile marathon Vs. Fail on a first date with someone who doesn't like pizza!?

I could go on for hours but I won't. I want to get to the good stuff. The bottom line is this. Tell them good or bad and tell them quickly. Rejection in dating is the best and quickest thing, you shouldn't avoid and it's easier and far more manageable than most other areas of failure and rejection in your own life. Welcome it with open arms. Be part of our generation's solution and not the problem. Let's change shitty dating once and for all! You with me? Then read (listen) on!

Life is too short. Yes, we've heard this so many times before but let me add it to being honest on the first date. Life's too short so stop wasting people's time. Life's too short so just be honest. Life's too short, so tell the other person how you feel. Life's too short so respect the other person's emotions. Life's too short so be considerate of someone's vulnerability. I could go on forever. But life is far too short. So do yourself a favor, LET THEM KNOW, GOOD OR BAD. Do NOT LEAD PEOPLE ON.

Yes you may or may not get rejected, also the world might end, you could get in a car accident, struck by lighting, robbed, house on fire, broken leg, and a bunch of bad shit. The worst things happen and will happen every year of your life. It's how you deal with it that counts. Life is 10% of things that happen and 90% of how you react or deal with it. So remember, you may very well get rejected or have zero sparks. I would expect it might happen, but be chuffed when it doesn't. Don't get me wrong 4 dates or more you might actually start liking the person. But in this current dating climate, as soon as people come they can go just as quickly. It's scary, sure, but you gotta be willing to get out there and go through it or you won't find your match. Whereas dating back in the day was like running on a lovely field assuming everyone had monogamous and good intentions (For the most part).

These days dating is like running through a bloody gauntlet, dodging people hurling fireballs at you on either side whilst trying to look for and find your mate. Now rejection is where you'll get hit by one of these fireballs so hard it will send you right on your back rolling around and writhing in pain ("Oh nooo I've been rejected ohhh nooo"). But if your emotionally tough. I mean really emotionally tough, you'll get up brush those ashes off, and start running again, stronger, faster, harder, tougher, and ready to punch those fireballs into a fucking oblivion. You got this! Remember this is not the worst thing to happen. But it is a chance to deal with it, learn from it, grow from it, move on and find someone significantly better. They got the jump on you! And that's okay, don't let your pride be a heavy determining factor on how you let this affect you. Maybe they realized that you two were not a good mix before you did, maybe they have their own issues to deal with, maybe they're seeing someone else. Either way, take it all in a large stride start making closer moves to your sweetheart.

TREY HAMILTON

19. Send Those Signals!

Courage, I realized, was not the absence of fear: it was the absence of selfishness; putting someone else's interest before one's own.

- **Michelle Cohen Corasanti**

Man or woman, you gotta let them know somehow. Yes, yes I know some of you might be old-fashioned and say the man should pursue. Fine, I'm at peace with that, but you gotta give the guy a clear-cut sign. Because men are not mind readers and neither are women. I know people are all about texting these days, I say give them a call and say, "Hey I got home, had a great time I'd love to do it again". If you're all about playing it cool, do it by text. Either way, if they don't get the message by then, they never will. Make sure you've expressed how you feel on your part and if it's not reciprocated at least you know you put yourself out there. They can deal with it. You want to make sure every interaction you have is positive and you can look back with no regrets with a clear head. Knowing that you have telegraphed your truth, they know how you feel. The fact they chose not to run with it, is of no reflection on you. That's true empowerment.

Do not play any games! (If you haven't already gathered, it's a major theme of this book) The whole playing it cool (low key) and not showing any interest to show interest is such nonsense, the biggest pile of bullshit I've ever had to withstand. The moment I know that's in motion with someone I'm trying to date I move, so fast my head spins. So do yourself a favor, if you really want to find love, stop it! Find that subtle way that works for you. If you are interested give them the green light to pursue. Give the look, the look that says. I kinda like you. Every now and then pause at the date, don't say a word and smile at them, then continue your sentence. Make it real with massive sex appeal, haha that was corny but it's true. But let's go a little deeper.

Much like the other key points in this book, they all require a little bit of understanding of the principle in itself. When you're sending signals you can't send too many and you can't send too little. You have to know that very, very small distance between coming on too strong and not coming off at all. There will be a great degree of trial and error but things like this make dating fun. They make dating become not something you dread but a rich internal and external interpersonal experience that can only help you to grow for the better. Like I always say though, people are so subjective in themselves that what one might consider sending too many signals the other person could say it's just right or not enough. So you have to connect and find a balance between what you're comfortable doing and what you know works. For example, a way I send a subtle signal is by reaffirming what I like in a potential partner after the person has described their character trait. I'll explain.

If a lady I'm with says, "I try to make sure I'm open and honest with how I feel when I'm dating someone." I would respond and say, "That's pretty cool, I really appreciate a woman who's confident enough in herself to try and be straightforward and honest with someone she's spending time with". See that! That right there is sending a signal. It's saying hey, "I like that! And I like you!"

But it doesn't have to just be audible signals. You can incorporate some physical signals too.

- When you gently touch the small of their back to guide them through a doorway
- You ask to take her bag to hang it up on the coat hanger. It's very simple but those are small signals
- A cute and quick tap on the shoulder after a funny moment has been shared
- You reach for the hand as you both slowly walk to the date location together (This is pretty forward but worth the risk)

I know what you're thinking. Wow, steady on here. Are these not a bit forward and aggressive? No way! No one has ever been arrested for any of the above issues on a first date. Especially if they've accepted the first date. If someone has openly accepted the first date with you, the odds are highly in your favor that they would be open to any of the following physical signals of attraction that you can send. Remember they have chosen to take time out of their day and life to spend time with you, they want to get to know you. What's the worst that could happen? You have to look for these opportunities where you can naturally send physical and audible signals that you are interested. Or that person might be clueless and put you in a zone. You know the zone I'm talking about. (Friend-zone)

Just so we're clear though there are some physical signals you could send that might possibly send that person running for the hills. They'd be telling anyone who can hear it that you are a creep! Trust me, people love explaining bad dating stories to everyone. You do not want to be the punchline.

a. **Desperate Dan** - You don't want to be that person who touches them non-stop because then it comes across as trying too hard and you look a little loved starved. They'll be sat there thinking, "what's this persons deal" Besides they'll be thinking you're trying to get the cow and milk for free. It's a dated analogy I know, but its archaic message still holds value.

b. **Eager beaver** - Just chill out. You have seen that message a few times here. I'll say it again. Just chill. Be careful not to come across as too eager. It's kind of like when you're just dying to get on that plane. But rather than waiting in an awkward huddle around the line like everyone else. Just wait for your seating zone to be read out. Then you may stand up and get in line like a normal person. You don't want the risk of them thinking you're just a muddling sex pest sending those signals so you can jump their bones as soon as the sun goes down.

c. **You're mine!** - We live in a generation where independent uniqueness and freedom of emotional possessiveness are celebrated. Let me tell you something, I am sooooo here for all that stuff. So be very careful not to send signals of possessiveness when you are on a first date. Trust me it happens more often than you think. I remember when I was talking to a work colleague at lunch. She told me about this terrible first date where they went to a restaurant. Apparently, the waiter was flirting with her a little as he was taken the order. Unfortunately rather than be a grounded man, the date she was with interrupted the waiter, "I'm sorry, she's with me. Just so you know". Holy shit! I wasn't even there for that. But man I feel uncomfortable.

20. Have A Pre-Game Before The Date!

I know I know, the whole process of trying to figure someone out before a first date is awkward. But it doesn't have to be. Before you go out with someone you want to get a good idea of who they are before you get yourself in either a good situation or a bad one. Are they extroverted? Introverted, talkers, polite, good at communication, funny, friendly, passive, and the list goes on. But that's something you most definitely want to figure out and figure it out ASAP. Like I keep saying, time is so valuable. So spend it with someone who is worth it. But how do you know, right? How can you possibly find these things out?

Well, a long time ago in a place far, far away they had these things called phones. Yes, I know you have one, but it was different back then. Apparently, they'd call you up before a date. Then they would get to know you over the phone for at least a couple of minutes. Everyone was doing it back then, "Phone calls". One day it all slowly started to fade away and the notion of calling before a date vanished. Eventually, people preferred sending letters through a screen rather than actually enjoying speaking to a real live human being. So yes, you can actually have a conversation on the phone. Why the hell not right? If you have anxiety talking to someone over the phone you had better get over it. Because in order to get what you truly desire you have to start by doing small things that make you slightly uncomfortable, things that force you to crawl out of that comfort zone and really start going for it! Ya know? If having a small chat on the phone is one of them. You're good to go!

I've read a few articles that swear you should rarely text before the first date or it will ruin the mystique. Just another kooky gamey article that wants to further the idea that we should play games before and while we're at the date. If you text a little before the date and the person feels like you're "giving them too much information". Fuck em. Who doesn't want to get to know someone? It's nonsense. I actually believe you can get to a better connection level when you do little prep work. It's like before you workout, you do a little stretch, drink a little water, maybe eat a small portion of fruit. Get your body in motion a little. Think of that as you're calling or texting before the date. It makes it far less awkward when you finally meet. Picture this:

Her: So how are Scrappy and Dougy?

Him: They're doing really well, I got them both doggy sandals today at Target

(Shout out to the guy who's ballsy enough to tell a woman he got his dog, "doggy sandals")

Picture that in your mind VS:

Her: So you got dogs right? I think I saw them on your Facebook?

Him: Yeah I do, two of them

This conversation above isn't bad. But the first conversation has more of a personal touch because a bit of light prep work has been done. They knew about their dogs because they had a previous light conversation. You can still prod for small facets of information via text to increase an air of familiarity. A phone call, however, heightens the chances for you both to be far more comfortable.

The other solutions are skype or facetime if you want to completely throw the comfort zone out the window! Or you can default to text. Not a bad thing by any means. But you can't as easily find out who a person is through text.

Look at this text thread for example:

Her: Do you like Iron and Wine?

Him : (**Search's Spotify, finds the top 5 most streams**) Yeah my favorite is "Flightless Bird".

See how easy that is to lie about? That's what text can do.

Imagine asking me if I've ever heard of "Phantogram" ". If i was there I'd look gormless and I'd say, "No". But if it's via text all I have to do is look it up and respond, "Yeah I like them, my favorite song is "I know nothing". My point being is through text people can be who they want to be. But vocally, that's who they truly are, they have to think on the spot and can't hide behind a whole web of information. Don't worry I get it, for some of you, you'd much rather have a conversation face to face rather than on the phone. But ask yourself this question. Would you rather risk having a crappy conversation face to face because you didn't weed them out? Or have an amazing conversation because you got a good vibe from a simple 10 - 15 minute conversation. Make sure this person is worth your time with a few simple questions.

There are also sneaky online tricks you can do to research someone and do a little background check. You know the usual, Facebook, Instagram, Linkedin, Twitter, and all that good stuff. But please ask for consent before you stalk them. It rubs some people the wrong way if you don't. I remember a friend of mine told me this horrific story. Essentially she looked up this super cute guy she was interested in. Her words, not mine. She looked up his Twitter and was greeted by super homophobic and racist memes and jokes. Sufficeth to say, this man did not get the first date.

But that's what I mean sometimes you don't even have to meet someone to know that something isn't right so be careful and always go by your gut instincts. The fact is any prep work you do can help get a better understanding of who this person is so you can feel significantly better about this potential date.

21. Meet At The Location (Be Careful)

"The danger which is least expected soonest comes to us."

– **Voltaire**

Dating these days can be sketchier than ever. Fake profiles, creepy Ubers, being groped in a bar, walks home at night, going to a sketchy part of town and the list goes on. So do yourself a favor and avoid meeting at their place or allowing them to pick you up. Until you've had at least one date, it's just not worth it. Could you imagine being picked up and the person is a complete dud? Boring as hell on top of that they drive like a maniac. Not a fun date. Furthermore, you meet at their place and they greet you with nipple clamps or some other kinky stuff. One of my friends told me of a story when she agreed to meet a guy at his place so they could ride together and grab a bite to eat. After 2 minutes of entering he said, "I'm gonna need you to take your top off, now." You can guess how that date went down. Meeting in a good, public central location is great for both parties. On the first date, you want to be as equal as you possibly can and set the stage for how the potential relationship would flourish in the future.

It's always better to be safe than sorry. Don't get me wrong, I'm not suggesting you board yourself up in the house and swear off dating out of sheer fear. But what I'm saying is this, would you rather be tortured in a basement or meet at a local coffee shop? Stuffed in a box and shipped to another country or have nice ice cream. You choose. But do not go to this persons home on the first date. I seriously can't fathom people who meet at someone's house for the first date and then say they had no idea the other person was going to try and jump their bones. Let's be real people we are humans we know how people's minds work.

You know all the classic tropes, tell the person where you are. Your closest friend maybe even two close friends. You should leave a moderate bread crumb as to what your plans are. For example, if you're going to meet at a location. Always ask for the address to be texted to you. So if you do go missing it gives people a good paper trail as to where to start looking. Wait, pause. The chances of these things actually happening are highly unlikely. But you always have to have your bases covered. Trust me, your mum will thank you for it.

Just be real, if your date suggests coming to his/her place before you've ever met. Just tell them, "I'm a little uncomfortable with this". Honesty and moderate vulnerability will always be the best state of play here. Trust me. If this book saves your life alone that's a win for me. Now if you start feeling some flickers of attraction and want to move it to a slightly more intimate location. You can, but I would strongly advise you have at least one or two more people in earshot. For example. The coffee shop gets a little stuffy. Go for a walk down the street, there may not be that many people there but there's the odd dog, windows slightly open, walkers, and joggers. This scenario allows conversations, not in earshot of someone drinking their pumpkin spice latte. But at least a small multitude of people where if you had to scream for help. They'd hear you.

Be sober on the date, one drink is perfectly fine. But anything after that only increases the danger for you. Plus who wants to be a sloppy drunk on the first date, it lowers your defenses and makes you more physically vulnerable. Just do things that put you in a far better space to be safe.

I'm gonna assume most people here have dabbled in online dating and even if you haven't how well do you really know someone? So until you feel comfortable you gotta watch your back, especially on the first date!

Emergency texts and travel arrangements always prepare for this. Always. Be careful. People just need one excuse to enact their crazy bullshit. Like I've said a million times it never hurts to be careful.

If someone says for a first date, "Yeah come over to my place and we'll "chill".

Remember. Don't do it! Please don't. No good can come of this. Especially if you don't know that person. Be careful. In my honest opinion, they're seeking intimacy before anything has really transpired and no good can come of that on the first date unless it's spontaneous and you've at least already met the person.

With technology these days there are so many measures you can take to make sure you're safe so utilize them. I wouldn't go crazy (call his boss, add his mum as a friend on Facebook, call her sisters, and all that stuff) But just make sure your bases are covered. Things like "find my iphone" or the find my friend's app and Facebook locator are the options you have to utilize so you feel confident that whatever happens you have prepared for the worst case. I would even suggest texting a friend when you get back too. Also, text your friends if you decide you are going back to this person's place. All easy and safe precautions. I want you to enjoy the first date, but I always want you to be a little aware. It never hurts.

Usually there are signs of it being a pretty bad date and we ignore it because we're so hopefully optimistic and eager to find the one we're looking for. So watch out for pre-date signs that might be a moderate red flag. For example.

1. If you've met the person online and they refuse to send you a picture for your contacts. They tell you, "just take a picture from my profile". That doesn't mean they're a serial killer. But why are they so resistant and how recent are those photos?

2. If they keep bringing up sexual topics via text (Before you've even met!? Really? Yeah that person is one-track-minded) If that's your bag, fair enough. I love sex a lot too. But if that's all they keep alluding to. Don't meet them.

3. They refuse to meet you in the middle for a date. You must come to their area. Urgh, selfish.

4. They want the first date to be at their place, to "Watch a movie"

Again, don't get yourself all paranoid and scared. But just be cognizant of all that's happening around you. I hear of too many stories that break my heart and I really don't want that to happen to you.

22. Leave Your Phone In Your Damn Pocket!

"What you do with your attention is in the end what you do with your life."

—**John Green**

The date is going well, he's looking at your eyes and you're looking at his, then bam! He pulls out his phone and checks a message. 20 minutes later it goes off and he says, "I have to get it".

Now don't get me wrong, his grandma could have fallen down and can't get up or something else dramatic. But I'm not really a believer in coincidences so I would avoid taking your phone out, ever. Put it on silent, put it away in your pocket, and focus on your date. I think the only time you should really whip it out is if you need an escape plan.

Be romantic let your life wait just for an hour or two whilst you enjoy the company of your date. It's the respectful thing to do and an unofficial thank you for your date taking their time to come and meet you. Being in the moment and present is something that our generation really struggles with. We gotta take pictures and record everything, we gotta tweet, post, and comment. But for those small moments be with that person and let them know you're there for them just by leaving technology alone for a few hours. If you're not already doing something such as this, try and let me know your results on my blog (Thefirstdatefix.com), when you decide to disconnect from technology and focus on your date you'll always get better results.

Putting your cell phone on the table on the first date just passively shows your social network and friends circle all in one fell swoop. Just keep it in your pants. (See what I did there) Imagine you're watching a movie and every 20 minutes it just stops. Then resumes 3 minutes later. Would you like that?! Hell no. So don't keep jumping to your phone. Just wait. Your date is free to do that if they so wish. But you won't!

If you're a doctor or something by all means you can, but just let them know beforehand. I dated a doctor once and she said before we even sat down, "Just so you know I'm on call so if I have to take a call I hope it doesn't offend you". I loved it, such a classy touch. Be honest about small things. It gives such a high level of interpersonal credibility to the interaction.

I get it though we're all glued to our phones. But for 1 hour, just one, learn to put it away. You can check to see if there's been a tsunami or earthquake later. There's nothing more offensive than when you're talking to someone and they're looking at their phone. Even when you're with a group of 3 - 4 people and you whip your phone out it's a little rude. But I'm old school like that. Like I said it's pretty self-explanatory. When someone creepily starts texting on a date it's saying "I have a little secret that you don't know about and you can't see". Granted in any other normal setting this would seem normal. But when you've first met someone they could be thinking a myriad of things if you don't give your texting some context. Here are some common thoughts that someone may have if you're texting on a first date

- Oh shit, are they texting about me!?
- What the hell!?
- Odd
- Man, am I that boring?
- Who could they possibly be texting right now
- Oh no, they're gonna tell me they gotta go
- Asshole
- They're setting up another date!
- I bet they're texting their ex!
- I'm never going out with them again
- Rude!
- Is everything okay?
- What did I do!?
- WTF?

These are just a few thoughts that they may be going through. Do not be the source of someone's slight first date anxiety issues, trust me. Have you ever hung out with a person who has a nervous tick or movement, just kinda moving around like they're waiting for their next fix. Yeah, that's you when you keep pulling out your damn phone. Cut that shit out, you're not that important. You agreed to meet them for an hour or two, so give them your unadulterated time and allow your whole self to be fully present. If you really want to be the cause of frustration that the other person may feel, then go ahead. But interested or not let's have and share positive interactions with the opposite sex. Please. Let's try and make every dating experience a good one and really be the change we want. Let's change those conflicted minds that are filled with thoughts of being deeply jaded. Like I said communication beforehand or after the fact will always go over well. Who would be offended if someone prepared you and said, "Hey I might go outside in the middle of this movie to take a call from my mum, she's moving today and it's a madhouse at the moment". Be as transparent as your possibly can and don't mess with people. Communication and honesty with the use of your cell phone will garner you the respect you want.

23. Master The Art Of The Four Seasons

In each season you are laden with perfect opportunities to capitalize on date ideas and make it a memorable experience for both parties. Some examples. Fall: haunted houses, Halloween parties, pumpkin patch, carve pumpkins, and a hike in the autumn leaves. Winter: ice skating, putting up a Xmas tree, Christmas shows in the theater, Christmas concerts, hot cocoa and a walk, snowboarding, snowshoeing. Summer, outdoor cinema, outdoor concerts, bike rides, long day hikes, swimming, beach, art festivals, laying out in the hammock you get the main gist here but try and plan awesome activities around what time of the year it is. Make sure you keep this in mind when your planning this incredible first date.

All you really have to do is get a good grasp of what season you're in. For example, if your in October, take them to a haunted house and get the pants scared off you. Then you both have great memories of when one of you lost your voice from screaming so loud, or your t-shirt was wretched in sweat because you were incredibly frightened. Now granted you can't talk in the horror house. But who doesn't want to discuss how awesome the haunted house was once you both leave. That's a great discussion point. Or you could have a date where you walk through the local park and admire the coloration of the leaves about to fall. Perhaps you even share an intimate moment as one of you laments a deep passion and connection you feel to nature.

There are some truly magnificent set pieces you can both go through together on one fine day. Just think about all the possibilities. Feeling like a haunted house is too much then why not carve some pumpkins together. One of you could be the Andy Warhol of pumpkin carving whilst the other is shit. Kidding. Or you could both be terrible and laugh at how ludicrously atrocious your pumpkins are. Still, feeling the buzz? How about a mid-fall afternoon hike. You might have the chance to hold hands, how romantic. Statistically fall is the best time to go out and get your date on.

Winter rolls around. Oh no, it's too cold to go out and actually enjoy the weather. Wrong. The winter season is when you can wear your best clothes and you can layer them. So no matter how shit the date is, at least you look good. So let's break it down for the winter. It's far more than cuddling up and watching some quality Netflix (Not a bad idea but I very much doubt anyone wants to do that on a first date). If Netflix is what's offered you can pretty much guarantee someone will be trying to swing their meat and two veg right in your face. Avoid it. You can go ice skating together instead. Another sneaky opportunity to do that classic hand holding if both of you click. You can be a gentleman and pick her up as she falls. Or you can be a lady and guide his nobly knees as he nervously skates along. Or your both former Olympic pros running rings around people and doing double pirouettes in the air. After 30 minutes people watching as you both enjoy that hot chocolate with just the right amount of sugar and cream. She raises the hot chocolate and has cream on her upper lip. You chivalrously get a napkin and wipe it off. You're both feeling that lightly dusted physical chemistry sprinkled around your whole night. He takes a big gulp of the piping hot chocolate and stutters as it's very hot and he just couldn't wait. You chuckle and laugh at his cute vulnerability. As you walk to the car his hands are shivering. But he insists that he doesn't want your hands to freeze so he wants you to keep your gloves on. You adore that, so you give him one glove. You both use each other's left hands for hand-holding and your right-hand slips in your pocket.

Maybe you kiss at the car. Maybe you kiss on the way. Maybe you don't kiss at all. Either way, this can be a perfect winter date. It sounds corny it sounds like a rom-com but this is a story someone told me. It happened. So it can very much happen to you. Not in the exact same way obviously. But you can still create those moments by strategically planning around those seasons. I myself have been a very happy recipient of someone planning a good date around the winter season and let me tell you. It made me fall for her pretty hard because I adored the time and effort she took into planning the date.

Spring. You invite them over for some spring cleaning. How romantic. Haha, no.

Perhaps you go strawberry picking. You go on an easter egg hunt. You can enjoy a romantic picnic. You can have a breezy trip on a paddleboat. Then feed the ducks at the pond. Suddenly one of them gets a little anxious and starts to eat the other duck's food. The duck scampers up to other ducks, chest puffed out as he meticulously devours their snack. The two of you giggle like school kids at the sheer cheekiness of this duck. Yeah, he's naughty but good grief is it funny. Suddenly the duck makes way for you and starts quacking at you nefariously.

You guys start slowly inching back but this big beaked bastard will not quit. He's on a mission, destroy the first date or die trying! Suddenly the park keeper comes along and warmly scolds you about feeding the ducks. The two of you laugh it off. Then the wise old park keeper begins to tell you about his first date with his late wife. You're both inspired and touched by this incredible story and sit gazed eyes at the remarkable tale of how genuine and sincere some relationships used to be. The park keepers walks away and wishes you both well on your first date. You both thank him and talk about what kind of time it must have been back then to date as you slowly walk around the park and take in the beauty of the buds of May. This date is bliss. You spot a gazebo in the middle of the pond. There's a cute young couple with a 3-year-old running around with a golden retriever and living her best life. You both connect on your love of dogs. He explains his dog died 4 years ago and he's only just gotten a new dog. You explain how your dog is blind in one eye and is in his last years. Then you both discuss your dream dog family, this conversation is going swimmingly. The sun starts to slowly go down. You really shouldn't waste this opportunity. A light kiss to the forehead or full tongue and the start of something effortlessly epic begins. You both know it.

You can both feel it.

You see! Again this is just simply planning around the kind of season you're having. You can create experiences just by planning around the seasons. Now don't get me wrong, not all first dates will be amazing like the ones I've referenced regardless of what season you're in. But it sure does increase your chances even if by a little it's always worth it. Remember the beauty of any date will always be in the effort from both parties. That's where you still get a satisfactory feeling whether it goes in your favor or not. The fact of the matter is this, you'll never regret a positive experience and making someone's day a little better even if you guys don't end up romantically connected. Where the negativity comes from is your reaction or lack of communication after the fact. If one of you isn't interested and doesn't notify the person, that makes a once positive experience a minor negative one. So be very clear, respectfully from start to finish.

Always plan around the time of year. Always try and get just a little creative. You can create moments you never quite knew were possible.

TREY HAMILTON

24. The 3Rd Date Rule

Ah yes, the thing we're all biologically programmed to want and desire but we have to pretend like we don't want it in public. It's taboo! We're puritans in public but super freaks in private. Never to be spoken at work and only reserved for certain conversational scenarios.

Well, you know what, I think that's all a load of rubbish. Absolute codswallop.

Should you talk about sex on the first date? Meh, there's no perfect answer to that. But I wouldn't rule it out. You are both adults and unless one person objects I wouldn't decide not to talk about it. But it's not something that should be forced. The conversation needs to arise naturally. For example:

Him: She was a bad kisser

Her: Yeah that probably means the sex would have been bad too.

You both erupt into laughter and continue talking about something else.

Scenario two:

Him: So what's your favorite position?

Her: Excuse me!?

Him: You know, how do you like to shag?

Two extremes yes. But it happens.

So should you wait for a few dates or just go at it on the first date. Again I don't think there's a right or wrong answer quite frankly. People have slept with each other after they have engaged in little more than 10 minutes of barely intelligible conversation in a bar, let alone a 2-hour stimulating conversation. Which would you prefer? It all comes down to individual preference and the best mutual consensual experience. But it doesn't have to be either-or.

(It definitely has to be consensual)

It's different for both parties though. If you're a woman you may not want to be labeled as a slut and you might actually want to meet the person again your paradigm will be slightly different than that of a man. If you're a man I would imagine you'd be a bit more open to sex on the first date. Cause unfortunately society has given men a get out of jail free card when it comes to first-time sex, first date sex gives you the label of "stud". Then the poor women out there are labeled hoes. It's actually still super messed up, but I think things are changing.

We all know some of the preconceived notions of sex when it comes to men and women right? People claim that men will lie about their aspirations to find love to get sex right? The opposite is said for women. Some people would tell you that women will lie about their views on sex to get love or affection from men. But the sad thing is, none of these are true anymore. Especially not in 2022 or if they ever really were true. We gotta stop furthering these generalizations of both men and women. It makes physical intimacy far more complex than it needs to be, for some people. Anxiety lurks around the corner ready to pounce at any moment when it only furthers how emotionally deep the situation already is.

There is not nor will there ever be a perfect time to get to know someone a little and make sure you at least have a physical connection. Dating for 4 months and then having someone end up being an utter disappointment in the sack is not a good look. When you have sex it's such a strong physical and emotional experience with someone, it's a connection that can't quite be explained. With sex, comes feelings and it will be hard for some people not to want to go further in the relationship. I suggest this unless you actually see something happening with a person or at least you want to be dating for a few months take great consideration as to who you sleep with. But if you are both adults and can clearly communicate what this is. Then go at it like lions in heat. These days some people operate backward with their mindset. If they really like the person they want to drag it out. But if they don't care about you, they want to hit and quit as soon as possible. Doesn't make any sense.

People should put themselves in a mindset where there are essentially no "3rd" date rules. It just makes things far more natural if you and your romantic interest are open to how you feel in the moment rather than some prescribed societal myth that you've volunteered to abide by. Remember there are no laws on when you both choose to have sex. None. The myth that scares "good boys" and "good girls" to hold out is just that. A myth. I say throw caution to the wind and do what feels right. I would suggest giving yourself your own "intimacy mantra". For example, your first line should be "I will only have sex, if".

I will only have sex if -

1. There's a huge connection, emotionally and possibly physically

2. I trust the person enough to share that moment with them

3. I at least know their first and last name

4. I've met their dog

5. It feels right

6. I fully expect to see them again and would like to start dating them exclusively

7. I feel very comfortable around them like I've known them forever

8. They're hot

9. I'm trying to get a green card

10. We both like Drake

11. I have a feeling it will be amazing.

These are just a few, some of them are thrown away statements but you get the gist. Just go by your OWN set of standards and above all else make sure the person is as close to the same page as you can get when it comes to sex. It won't always be the case but you'd be surprised. I once had someone tell me that they were okay with having sex. But they don't kiss cause it's a sign of commitment. I kid you not!

To be honest, though, it's all so subjective right? People out there love to play a coy, good, chaste person role until they're fully ready to let loose. That's not an issue. But again, why hold off so long? Then you've got people who after an hour of meeting you, want to rip your clothes off. Neither is bad. Especially if you hold yourself by your own rules and your own accountability. Not what your parents say, not what the media and society have taught you. But by YOUR own rules and standards. But if you're under 18. Listen to your parents, they know best.

I know, I know. There are people who might have bedded you in a new york minute and then vanished without a trace. Fine, it happened. You gotta be a grounded individual dust it off and move, again it's far more of a reflection on them as opposed to who you are. But I'm telling you this right now. Those people will always be there. I've heard and had stories where the person has held out for 2-3 months or so. The reason being is because previously when they went with their emotions and what felt right for them, it didn't go their way after the fact. Meaning as soon as the other person in the relationship got their sex, they vanished! By 3 months feelings would have definitely occurred. Unless you're a gargoyle with a heart of stone. You would have developed some pretty raw emotions with that person and I might go as far to say, possibly saw a future. But what if you're were the person who had sex on the 2nd or 3rd date. Not that many feelings and not that much emotion after that number of dates. So it's a question of which you would prefer, obviously those are two extremes but often that's how it very well might be.

Either way no matter the time when you sleep with someone, they could still end up ghosting you and becoming a "missing persons" in your life. So the "number of dates" rule needs to end. You need to have more than a rule of time that separates your decision on intimacy. It needs to come from a deep-rooted value system and ideological paradigm to which you have tried and tested and you feel like it's the sweet spot for future success for you and that lucky person. For other people who vocalize their rule of time, it could be a little frustrating. You're sat there saying to yourself, well the last time I let my emotions lead the way they really hurt me and they ran off as soon as they got what they wanted. Remember my chapter previously, "Just be because you tripped over running, doesn't mean it's going to happen all the time you run". A lot of reasons why some dates are doomed before they even begin is because people are stockpiling. Stockpiling emotions and baggage from previous relationships. It's fine to have a little apprehension. But what's not fine is projecting your fears onto someone else when they've given you no reason to do so.

I once had a friend who told me this story which I thought was so backward. She had explained to me that she and this guy had an amazing connection. They laughed a lot with each other, they opened up and were vulnerable. They seemed to effortlessly connect and things were very natural and organic.

One night things got hot and heavy. The guy pulled back. They sat there for a few minutes watching TV. Then she broke down and a conversation ensued.

Her: What's wrong?

Him: Oh nothing I just usually don't go that far after a first date

Her: Oh I'm sorry

Him: No I'm sorry, I just usually wait till the 7th date or so before I'm ready for that

Her: Oh, okay.

Him: Sorry. Maybe I should explain.

She looks at him with a little puzzled gaze. She's feeling very awkward and slightly uncomfortable.

Her: Okay.

Him: Well once I was seeing this girl, for a bit. After the first date, we slept together. We hung out a few times after that up to the 4th date. But she seemed different. A little off, you know? Anyway, long story short after we went to dinner on that 4th date I text her and let her know I wanted to see her again and she ghosted me. I even text the next day. Nothing.

Her: I'm really sorry Paul, that sucks. You seem like such a good guy.

Him: Thanks, but that's why I don't like to rush things. Especially with you, I actually really like you, and I haven't really got along with anyone like this in a while.

Her: Yeah that's totally fine.

It wasn't fine.

I remember when we all discussed this at our Harry Potter book club (Yeah I know, but HP is dope, don't hate. Appreciate) She randomly brought it up with 3 of us from the group afterward. I remember how confused she was. She just didn't get it. It felt kinda pre-prescribed to her. Like on the 7th date, here we goooo! Sex time. There was nothing natural or romantic about that. It's scheduling an appointment. The only time it's fairly okay to schedule sex is when you've been married for 10+ years and it's the only time the kids will be away and when your work schedules and other commitments are free. Her attraction dimmed and she was very, very turned off. Not because the guy was honest, if anything she appreciated that. But because she disagreed with it. Unlike the other girl, my friend literally admitted that she felt a stronger connection, liked him and sees a potential future? So why was she being passively held back by the actions of a previous woman? Why was she put into the same bucket as someone who would do something like that? It never really worked out with the two of them. I don't think that guy was wrong with his beliefs. There will definitely be someone that honors his rules. But for my friend, it just kinda changed her attraction completely. She didn't feel like he was emotionally mature enough to take a chance and risk on. Her principles were based on her valuing emotional risks and being free to make the decisions you want to regardless of the past. That's why we're good friends!

But I do understand, I truly empathize. There are a lot of people who are very sensitive about the time they have sex with people and you have every right to feel that way. My main point here is to make sure you're considerate of your own feelings. Whilst also having a clear understanding that making your decision on consensual sex, shouldn't be purely timeline-based. That's only a small factor in this decision you make and needs to be far more magnified. Don't make decisions about sex based on someone else's opinion or what Vogue, Cosmopolitan, and Men's Fitness tell you. Live happily and confidently by your own rules, be very safe and go with the flow that feels as real as possible.

Be wary of other people's opinions when it comes to this. Believe it or not, conflicting views about values when it comes to sex really have to be aligned. For example, there could be someone who only has sex when they're in a committed relationship. Nothing wrong with that, but then you have to remember that not everyone shares the same opinion. So if it means holding out until someone's on that same level so be it. You can't feel upset if someone your dating isn't wired that way. That's where a little bit of communication goes a long way

Your sexual values must not be based on a source of fear. Fear of rejection, fear of abuse, fear of the outcome, and external safeguarding. I once was on a date with someone who didn't have sex because her ex-husband was a physical abuser and used sex for gain for himself rather than a shared experience. I felt so bad for her especially since I really cared about her and was pretty upset anyone would ever treat her that way. The problem was though because of that she was scared to open up sexually. Which meant there were cuts too deep to really move forward with. Not a bad thing by any means.

But it's like I said at the beginning of the book. You have to be ready for all those things before you date. Emotional baggage is something everyone possesses. You have every right to carry it, everyone does. What isn't healthy though, is allowing that previous pain and baggage from past relationships and marriages to affect how you open yourself up. Sure the argument can be made that if they truly love you, they'll wait and be there for you. But in the beginning stages of dating that's far too much of an emotional investment to ask from anyone especially when they don't quite know you enough. So if your one person reading this who has held out for so long because of things in your past, it's okay to feel pain. But don't let it affect your future with a new potential person. If you're still struggling with it, there are people you can see. Love scars affect people in different ways.

Decades of books, movies, and "self-help books" have lied to you. The whole one-dimensional mindset, if you do things this or that way you'll get everything you want, is garbage. Sure there are moderate guidelines you should follow (This book ;)) But for the most part. Have a blueprint and build the whole damn house yourself. No advice in the world can stop or save you from having sex with someone who has ill intentions, those people are always going to be around. Urgh, they feed off nice vulnerable people like us. Those callus and cowardly people who can't tell you what they really want.

They can take a long walk off of the shortest pier ever created. I prefer people who are direct and blunt. I have so many friends who complain about things like this, "He sent me a message saying I want to bang your brains out" . Sure it's direct and kinda lewd. But at least that person is honest and now my friend can choose to ignore or accept such a brazen and classless invitation. She knows right there and then what this scrub's intentions are. Rather than some "sneaky pete" who swears he wants something serious and soon as he gets sex. He's out. I'm telling you right now and again, these people are either gonna run off like a thief in the night or they won't. But if you at least have your own rules and stick to those you won't feel as cheated.

I dug around a little and read a few articles and books about this subject. There was a study conducted by using 2000 people and apparently dating and having sex after the 3rd date is a dated notion. For some people, it's actually longer! Yeah, you heard me right. Us Millenials are not as bad and as sexually promiscuous as other people say.

The results of this 2000 people survey suggested that the average person would wait for the 9th date before letting their clothes drop to the floor and playing some Ed Sheeran. This was a study completed by Groupon. Yes, Groupon. Apparently, the authority on all things sex right? Either way, they pulled some very interesting pieces of information. The guys in this study felt like any date after date 3 is appropriate to start creating that sex playlist on Spotify. Women in the study felt like the 9th date was appropriate to start wearing those matching pieces of underwear. 30% of men and 8% of women agreed that sex could happen from 1-3 dates. Interesting. Very interesting.

Sex, sex, and more sex! But there are different levels of intimacy. What about first kisses. Those things that some people dream of in the right "circumstances". Results from the survey found that some people don't kiss till the 2nd date. The chemistry could be more alive than a Mythbusters episode but they still wait till the 2nd date. Bonkers! That's 17% of 2000 people who always kiss on the first date. The other 83% what do they say? Well 39% will definitely close their eyes and await a mutual massaging of lips (Woohoo!) But the other whopping 45% say, NAH. That shit ain't happening! I'm sure none of these results are shocking, right?

But where does age play in these intimate scenarios? Well according to the survey the younger you are the more likely you are to swoop in and kick the chemistry meter up a notch. Might be because they've been burned fewer times. Unfortunately, the older people get the more jaded they become. More on that later...

But who makes the first move eh? Who's the person that risks it all and could face a hefty rejection. It's 2022 and it's still the man who has to go in for the first kiss. A measly 3% of women feel like they should be the ones to initiate a kiss. Haha so like it or lump in men. We gotta pull up those big boy pants and romance these ladies (Consensually of course).

So until you at least have a rough idea of where you want to take it with any person, be patient and keep it in your pants! It's not just about knowing where you want to take it but it's about knowing where you stand. If the two of you are not sincere with where you're both at in terms of how you feel, be very careful. I say this because if you don't know how many people they're seeing besides you they could have multiple sex partners and you do not want to be in that rotation. So another thing I'd recommend is asking them, so how many other people are you seeing right now. To be honest, you can say it whenever you like, I couldn't care less. If I was on a first date and someone asked me that, I'd respect them. I'd think it was ballsy as hell but they want to know where they stand. I like that. If you however are so sexually turned on you want to live by your own rule of throwing caution to the wind, by all means, you can. But be prepared to deal with things that may not go in your favor.

25. They're Not My Type!?

This phrase is one of the most annoying phrases I have ever heard! I swear to god. What does that even mean? People who say that are usually in two different camps.

The people that have a type and have never dated someone they might actually be extremely compatible with and occasionally date someone a little different.

Or the people who only date a "type" with the exact same specifications with each person they date. So they could be doomed to experience a crazy groundhog day whirlwind of bad dating experiences. But hey, "they have a type".

The definition of insanity is doing the same thing over and over again. If it's not working out with the "type" you keep going for. Why keep going for them? "Cause they're hot", right!? Urgh. C'mon now. You know, when they're in their 80's all you'll be left with is wrinkly tattoos of shit that used to be cool back in the day with super dated references and a personality that reeks so bad people still shudder of ever knowing that person that you decided to marry.

Okay, that was a little dramatic sure. But you gotta change it up a bit. So long as you're still attracted to the person go outside a little from your type. Start thinking about characteristics that might be far more beneficial down the line. Start thinking about things on a far more intellectual level and consider life choices and decisions they've made that have made them the person they are today. I know, when you go on a date you want to just be present and be in the moment. All this is true. But you still have to look at the big picture in my opinion. Or you're doomed to make the same mistakes with people who will be a fleeting moment in the story of your life. As much I encourage dating and experiencing what you're into and finding out who you are a little. You don't want a dating track record as long as a CVS receipt.

Need more advice. Look at it this way. If I'm a lady and I say I always date "artists". Let's say it doesn't always work out for me and these artists. Why would I keep going for them? Sure you could hit the relationship jackpot with one of them, but I doubt it would be because he's an artist.

If I'm a bloke and I say. I only date girls who are classy, rich, and super sophisticated. They gotta make at least 6 figures and some other trivial characteristics. But if all of those relationships with those types of women fail. Where does that leave me? It means I should look into deeper or perhaps more life-altering and effective character traits.

What do I mean? You ask.

Let me give you a few examples and preface them beforehand. If you're in a long-term relationship or marriage, which I assume is your long-term goal. Just think about the things that might arise in any of those two scenarios of either. Marriage, a Relationship, or even serious dating.

Examples :
- You/they lose their job
- Car accident

- Pregnancy
- Birth
- Job Promotion/Job demotion
- Shock medical diagnosis (MS/Cancer/Brain Damage etc)
- Fatality
- Family drama
- Seriously conflicting viewpoints
- Racial differences
- Politics
- Affection/displays of affection
- Money
- Communication
- Conflict Resolution
- Change of life choices
- Religion
- Weight gain/weight loss

The crazy thing is I've only really scratched the service of what people in those current circumstances might possibly go through. These are real issues and some of them are definitely going to affect you and your future love. So with that said how will these, let's call them "vanity characteristics" really help you get through the issues listed above:

- Artistic
- Sophisticated
- Tall
- Handsome
- Classy
- Fashionable
- Sexy
- Athletic
- Wears heels
- They can surf
- Listens to cool music
- Has cool friends
- Watches good tv-shows

- They like to camp
- They're outdoorsy

Now is there anything wrong with the above "vanity" characteristics? Hell no! They're some great things to have in a partner. But you shouldn't allow that to be the definition of your type. For example, Compare the previous issues one couple might face (Cancer, unemployment, etc) and compare it to some of the "Vanity" characteristics as previously stated. If you both have communication issues, which characteristic would best solve this? The fact they can surf? Oh wait they wear heels, or maybe the fact they're handsome what about them being tall, would that help? Not really. All those vanity characteristics serve no purpose in this particular scenario. Okay well, let's branch out a bit. What if you're having money problems in your relationship. It's okay, your spouse is tall right? No that won't work, mmmm they're in good shape. Nope, being in good shape isn't going to make money come from the sky. Unless you're a pro athlete anyway or have some cliched fitness Instagram page with 500k followers.

My point being is the previous characteristics are not bad by any means. But they should come secondary to the most important things. I truly believe looks are important for sure, I mean you want to wake up with someone and praise the greek gods they're even in your bed. But it's only a small portion in the grand scale of finding that special someone. After looks, you gotta start looking for and being attracted to people who have far more complexity in regards to who they are and what their character is. The very fiber of what they could possibly contribute to the relationship should be greatly considered. So whilst the second list I provided in this chapter is all good. Start thinking in a much wider spectrum and make sure that you start looking into other ways they might be your type. Consider other aspects of their personality as you continue to date them and the values that you both share. Consider some of these things:

- Upbringing
- Religious background
- Conflict resolution skills
- Reactions in a crisis
- Life values
- Patience
- Basic soft skills
- Political views
- Goals
- Dreams
- Independence
- Candor
- Authenticity
- Family relationships
- Friends and the company they keep
- Social EQ
- Work Ethic
- Common Sense

Do yourself a favor, forget the He's/She's/They're "not my type" nonsense. It will kill any chance of you finding true happiness I promise you. Open yourself up on a first date. Expand the possibilities of any real chance to be happy with someone. When you say you have a type, what you're doing subconsciously is eliminating more options, shrinking your dating pool if you will. Start thinking outside the box and genuinely trying to find out who they are and make it fun. I say, just so long as you're attracted to them whether they're your type or not. Just go in with no expectations and see where the date goes.

Relax and follow the flow of the river. There are a bunch of things that could go wrong on a date. But as long as it's nothing to do with your date and are aspects around the two of you that you can't control, that's where the brilliance lies. Don't let little things bug you. Enjoy their company. The grass is only greener where you water it, people. So when you're on that date, have a positive mindset and don't let the fact this dude wears stone-wash jeans or this girl wears a fanny pack distract you from how awesome they might be. Besides fanny packs are coming back!

26. Just As Important As The Entrance Is The Exit

"How lucky I am to have something that makes saying goodbye so hard." – **A.A. Milne**

I tell you what, I have left many a date awkward. I've driven off a few times thinking. "Shit! What happened, oh god why did I say that". You have to make sure you leave with the person wanting more or at least understanding how great you are. No one really thinks about it as they're so focused on making sure the actual date goes well.

The first thing you have to do is be clear when you leave that you'd like to see the person again. Trust me, in my research, there have been a few "gamey" articles that are convinced you shouldn't say a word till at least 48 hours in regards to asking for a 2nd date. I say, how dumb is that! It's so transparent too. People know you're playing games so why do it? Do not fall into the trap. None of this "maybe", situation. If you genuinely like them don't buy into the silliness of who has the power and dictates what happens next. Like I said people can really see what you're trying to do and it's very unattractive for the most part.

Chances are if they're the kind of person you could possibly see a dating future with they probably won't be in the mindset of playing games, most people of high emotional value usually aren't. I remember when I had a great date with someone and when I said, "I had a great time let's do this again". She responded, "I'm not sure. I'll let you know. I'm really busy the next 3 weeks". Was she interested? Was she not interested? Was she playing a game and trying to play it cool? Either way, it didn't matter by the time I arrived home I had already decided it was a no for me. Maybe, is so undefined. By definition alone, it screams of strong abstruseness. So if she didn't know, why would I pursue it? So I didn't. To be honest, as much as my ego doesn't want to hear this, she probably wasn't interested. Which is another reason why I'm writing this book. Let's change the narrative of dating and be a little more positively candid with people. Had she merely said, "I'd like to be friends"? Or, "I'm not sure if we'd be compatible". Shit, I would have taken it like a G and bounced. But she didn't and she left with obvious ambiguity. I could see people's slight apprehension about being a little candid. The person being rejected might react in a way that's a little intense. But like I said previously, the more you are honest with your date and yourself. The easier these experiences will be.

I had no regrets. I expressed that I wanted to see her again and the answer I received wasn't really an answer. So what do you do with that? Absolutely nothing, the moment someone hits you with a lick of vagueness you dust it off your shoulder and bounce. Flutter away like a feather gently breezing past in the wind. Cause you're worth more and should never be a small option or appetizer on the menu, you're the main course, you out here looking like a meal. So make sure you say it! If that's how you feel anyway. The mystery of who's interested after the date is one of the most annoying parts, some people legit get off with that. They love the game playing and "will they won't they" scenario. But that's problematic in itself. Cause once all of that is over and you are steadily dating in a relationship. Those are the same people who claim "the fire is gone". What they fail to realize is that the fire was only there because they both played games with each other, now they have what they wanted, game over. The thrill of chasing and chemicals running through their brain has settled, time to get real. That's the problem with games, especially dating games. Eventually, they have to end, there's usually a winner of a loser. The spice of uncertainty will run out, always.

Once the date is done if you'd like to see them again, be vocal about it. In most cases, you'll get the answer you want, whether it's what you'd like or not. If you're feeling like this person is not the person you'd like to continue seeing just say. "It was nice to meet you tonight, thanks for your time". Or something more catered to your personality. If they turn around and say, "I'd love to do this again". Politely thank them for their interest and let them know you'd like to be friends. If they don't get the hint then, they never will. But you must do everything you can to leave on a good note. Spread some good karma and don't allow the person to feel like shit just because you're not interested.

If you haven't already guessed. This book's main message is to think outside the box and do things a little differently. So one thing I would recommend is avoiding that cliche everyone says after the first date.

Try and implement what I like to call "future projections". Example: During the date, when you feel it's going well, say to them playfully: "Next time we have dinner, you order the wine," or "Next time we meet, we should see a movie, I bet you'll talk all the way through it." As you can tell, these examples have a playful undertone to them, but most importantly, they are **PRESUMING** that there will be another date without a flimsy question dangling at the end of it.

It's not cute to lead someone on! So don't do it. Please. You may lead them on because you don't want to be a bad person. But check this out, if you do lead them on, you ARE a bad person and a cowardly one at that.

Now if there are green flags on both sides there are a few ways you can leave it. You can go with a safe hug and the obligatory church double pat on the back. Kinda boring but it's the safe bet. No one gets offended or calls the police. If you want to throw a little caution to the wind, hug them just slightly longer. But I say if you're really getting good and consensual vibes of physical chemistry, go in for the kiss!

Yes, I know what you super classy people are saying reading this. "I never kiss on the first date". But why? Ask yourself that question what's so bad about that? It's not like you're sleeping together. It's an innocent first kiss to see if both of you have that physical chemistry too. It lets them know very immediately. "Hey, I like you and want to pursue this further".

Yes, they can reject you easily, and that's their right. But it's like anything else. Why play it safe? Take some risks and throw your whole damn body off the boat and in the ocean. None of this dipping your toes nonsense.

27. Don't Flake!

You've been texting this handsome gentleman all week, you've been sending silly memes, snaps of you singing in the car to your favorite Lady Gaga song, pictures of you out with your girls. He's been sending you pictures too, funny memes as well. You've both exchanged the obligatory good morning texts, or the "How's your day going texts," you know the ones I'm talking about. Now it's time today is the day, tonight will be the night. You may have even told one or two of your friends the excitement you have and moderate joy for meeting this fellow. Sure everyone swears they have "no expectations" but deep down you all have a tiny little desire that it might work out with this one or you wouldn't even show up. So the day is here, you leave work giddy and excited to finally meet this guy, 20 minutes before you're at the venue you feel a vibration in your pocket. You know it's the text notification. Your heart tenses up and a little, you have a feeling what it might read, you know the text I'm talking about. You pull over and read the text.

"I'm so sorry something came up (I'm sick, my mum's sick, I totally forgot, yada yada yada)"

Yep (sigh), you guessed it they flaked! They didn't show up, they bailed! Now for those of you who are good kind-hearted people who might not have felt the sting of being flaked on too many times. You might be thinking, "Wait now maybe he really did have something come up, maybe he is sick or his mum is sick or some other excuse he text, is actually true." I'm gonna level with you here people, they're probably lying! I know, I know. Other books have told you to look on the brighter side, to not take it personally, you don't know their circumstances, they're probably telling the truth and give them another chance. Guess what I say to that.

BULLSHIT.

Take it from me and you know this too. If you want to make time. You'll have time. It's that simple, this person doesn't give a shit about you or your time. They cancelled right before your date 20 minutes before. The chances of that happening are very very little. They just are. If I was Bill Gates and I turned around and made an announcement on Youtube and said, "The first person who meets me for a cup of coffee at (Your local starbucks) I'll give you 1 million dollars". Even if you had the flu, car broke down, no gas you were in a wheelchair, bullet to the leg, and blind in one eye you'd find a way of getting there! My point being is that if someone really wants to do something, they would. This is no new information for you. But you need to hear it in order for you to survive and be stronger emotionally in this dating world because the harsh light of day is this. People will lie to you and makeup excuses, sometimes because they don't know you well enough for the truth. Sometimes because they're just very inconsiderate. Some cause they don't give a shit.

I once held a focus group with about 20 women who were single mums. I was fascinated by some of their dating experiences. This one lady named Gina recounted a story where she traveled from her suburban home to meet a guy for drinks, downtown. Before doing so she had spent 40 dollars on a baby sister and got a new blouse as she was excited. The trip would take her about 30 minutes so she left 5 minutes earlier for contingency time. 15 minutes into her journey, the guy canceled. He canceled via text! What a prick. His reason? "He totally forgot that he had friends party to go to".

This person is just not interested. I say that much because there was a level of interest. They did text you, they did share jokes, they did send pictures. But when it came to crunch time and they had to meet with you, what did they do!? They bailed, dude. They gave you a lame excuse and couldn't even be bothered to be honest. You're still reading this thinking that they generally are for real, right? They probably really are sick, their cat really is lost, they totally did space on the time, they can't make it, they have to work late, they forgot about a friend's dinner and all those other lovely excuses you've either received or given. But how do you know if the person is for real maybe they really are sick or whatever other excuses they have? There are some methods you can use to weed this person out. The first would be our golden rule of this book. BE HONEST. For example a simple text like this.

Text No.1. "I'm sorry to hear that, I was looking forward to meeting you, but if you're not interested anymore that's okay too"

You're giving that person that cold honest truth and giving them a clear opportunity, to be honest, and genuine. There are a few ways this can go.

Scenario A - They respond and tell you they're totally still interested and try and reschedule at a later date. If they do this, they're worth one more shot in my opinion. Man or woman if you flake on the first date and you're still interested it's up to you to recover this and reschedule. The person who has been flaked on is well within their rights to allow you to put a bit of work in.

Scenario B - They respond defensively and are a little annoyed you were so straightforward. This is a person I would avoid if it gets contentious on their side just because you were honest with how you were feeling. This is an immediate red flag and someone who doesn't have the emotional maturity to engage in sincere texts is not an adult. You're just trying to find out where you stand. After all, they flaked on you. If they're offended with you trying to figure out where you stand. They're not suitable for any more time given. You can and will do better. Go get that hour back and watch a few episodes of Friends.

Scenario C - They don't even respond, nuff said.

Scenario D - They apologize profusely and give you more excuses. But they don't suggest a rain check and if they do, there is no date, no time, and no venue. This person is a jabroni and is wasting your time. They want someone to stroke their ego at a distance and will be happy to text you until you turn into a pumpkin. Reclaim your time!

<u>Text No1..</u> - "No worries"

That text right there is the guarded "I don't really care text". A lot of people would go with this. It's safe and would allow you to subtly save face and in the game-playing world of dating, I guess you'd be playing the whole "I don't really care" card. But you do care and you're only fooling yourself. Now you have no closure and you have no idea what really happened apart from the fact you were flaked on. Maybe you truly don't care and that's fine. But you get far more growth in the dating experience from being authentic with who you are and being honest with your emotions. The best thing you can do is leave a situation knowing you were honest and vulnerable with your head held high. I promise and know you'll garner much growth and truly be closer to finding that person who is inspired by and honors that small facet of who you are. There are a few ways they can respond to this.

Scenario A (Text 2) - They respond with a, "Okay, thanks a lot" If they respond with that and nothing more. They wanted an escape route and you politely gave it to them, now they can wash their hands of you. Great. Now you know their character and you can hop right off that boat with ease.

Scenario B (Text 2) - They respond a little condescending or nervously with, "Are you mad at me?" This is where it gets a little tricky. Cause responding to this could be like gas to fire and create an argument in itself and you haven't even met them yet. So you gotta think about this just a little. Like I keep saying, respond with honesty. In most cases, a 20-minute pre flake is a little disappointing. So let them know, you were a little disappointed. Remember life isn't always about what happens it's how you respond to it. The person's reactions to these texts will be the deciding factor as to whether you give them another shot if they're open to it at all.

The last text option you have would be to not even respond. A little petty IMO but at the same time if you honestly don't have the energy you don't have to respond. But remember you're different. You leave every interaction as well as you found it. You want your dating life to be as without blemish as much as possible. So whilst you have every right to ignore them, I recommend the vulnerable honest approach. You have nothing to lose but everything to gain.

Do you know what I'm looking for right now? My time to be wasted, gas to be squandered and someone to completely stand me up and flake on me. I seriously would love that, there's nothing better than having a long hard day at work, heading to a date only to be stood up. Anyone ever described that to you at great length? Anyone, anywhere? Exactly. No one wants their time to be wasted and no one wants their ego to bruise even a little. Just take that little paradigm of awareness and run with it. If you're wanting to flake. I would at least give them 6-12 hour notice bare minimum.

There's a difference between flaking and canceling the date.

Flaking = flaking on your date within 1-2 hours before you're scheduled to meet them

Canceling the date = Cancelling the date within an 12-24 hour period before the planned occasion. You can either re-schedule or be honest with why you'd not like to meet them

Be part of the solution. Not the problem! I'm sure you've sat there and complained to your friends about that jerk who stood you up and how bad it made you feel, how much you want that asshole to know how it feels. Do yourself a favor, do not project those emotions on someone else by doing the same thing. As far as you are concerned you're a person of your word. If you see some red flags and you really are not comfortable meeting the person. At least give them a 24- 12 hour heads up that you can't make it. Don't tell them 1 hour before the date. It's poor form and you're better than that. Be a person of your word, it's always odd to me when a person says yes to a date, knowing they're going to say no later. what's wrong with you!? I just always say to my friends. How would you feel if she did that to you? And the answer is usually very simple.

Don't flake!!

28. Beware The Overaction!

I'll never forget the time I was on a date and the person I was with didn't even know my name, haha shit makes me laugh when I think about it even now. Her rationale was if it didn't work out she didn't want to put a name to my number, highly unusual and a little morbid, but still kinda funny. If I can give you any single piece of advice it would be to remember the person's name and remember it well. Nothing says I respect you more when you actually remember the person's frickin name. So long story short she forgot my name and I reacted like a large majority of the dating population would.

"How can you forget my name?" I was in complete shock, "So you go on a date with someone without even knowing their name". Yep, I fell into that trap. When in reality like I keep remarking on every chapter or so, life is 10% what happens to you and 90% how you react. I didn't react terribly but I was clearly offended she saw it on my face, my intonation and general demeanor, completely changed. It was hard to bounce back from that. But to be honest I didn't much want to. In the sense that, who would want to date anyone who spends their own time going on a date and not even having the courtesy to remember someone's name. What a bloody waste of time. Highly irregular.

But be very careful how you react. Just be cool about it, take mental notes, and move on. For example, if someone turns around and mouths off some political opinions that you don't necessarily agree with. Don't react and go on the counteroffensive, we want positive first-date experiences. Instead ask them questions get where they're coming from, "what makes you support this particular political individual". When your instinct is to react to something you don't agree with or become frustrated with your date's views or opposing opinion just be cool calm and collective. You don't want to make it awkward more importantly.

What's the point? You may not agree but you can actually learn something from an opinion significantly different from yours. Above all else, it's their truth and something they stand by. So don't make them feel shitty just cause you think it's weird. Imagine this, you got on a date with this super amazing person, it's about the hour mark and they bring up the fact that this political person in mind actually has some great tax laws. You on the other hate that person, the political leader is a pedantic, megalomaniac who only cares about herself/himself. You lose your shit and proceed to ram your opinion down this person's throat about why they're wrong and they should change their mindset after you are done, they respond to you finally and say, "Yeah I actually agree, I just really like his/her tax laws". Boom finished. This person probably will not call you again, nor will they want your agenda shoved down their throat.

What is interesting about impulsive behavior is its difference dependent on sex. I.E men are far more likely to react to something they disagree with far more than a woman. This wasn't really news to me, but it might be to some of you men out there, whereas some women could be reading this having a slight chuckle to themselves, knowing that they have encountered this various times. In a study conducted by Jessica Weafer, P.h.D. and Harriet De Witt, Ph.D. They ascertain that there are significant differences in measures of impulsivity between men and women. Women discount more steeply than men. This means if either of you disagrees on something fairly strongly, typically but not always, the man will have a stronger reaction. Essentially men are much harder on the acceleration and women are much more prone to pump the brakes.

Christopher Badcock (It's his real name BTW, he's not a bond villain or a pornstar), author of The Imprinted Brain, attests that "sex differences in impulsiveness are seen more graphically on the road, where men drive more recklessly than women, are less likely to use seat-belts, and are more likely to speed, tailgate, refuse to yield, jump lights, and drive while drunk. The result is a male accident rate three times as high as that of females in the USA and a fatality rate higher (four per billion miles for a 33-year old female and 40 for a 20-year old male). Indeed, the courts find that men commit 97 percent of dangerous driving offenses, 85 percent of careless driving offenses, and 83 percent of speeding offenses. Another result is that men—and young men driving fast cars especially—can pay up to three times the insurance premiums of women of the same age".

That's absolutely bonkers when you think about it, but for me as a pretty led foot prone individual behind the wheel, it makes sense. Men reading this might be crying their male tears shaking their heads angrily and crying out, "What does this have to do with dating". It means you gotta pump the breaks, man. Anything you disagree with be careful and tread that line. Because the moment you start preaching and going off on one. It's very unattractive. You might be saying to yourself. "Yeah but that's who I am". That's all well and true but in the early stages of dating. The trust and rapport aren't nearly as strong enough to move past awkward conversational differences. They don't know you yet. They're not aware that there are so many better things about you despite the fact you could be over-opinionated.

So gentleman, do whatever you can to be a grounded man in your own life. When there are things you disagree with, try your best to remain calm, think a little, and then give your opinion if you feel the need to do so. Mastering this will make you far more prepared and calmer if there's something you disagree with on your date. There's nothing more attractive than a grounded man who disagrees in a way that's so classy and graceful that the person almost ends up agreeing with him because he translated his thoughts so well.

29. Are You A Kicked Dog?!

Are you a dog that's been kicked a little hard? Metaphorically speaking of course. If any of you have adopted an abused dog. You know those first couple of weeks, and months are hard for that poor little thing. sometimes they wince at a bare movement because they think you're going to reign some Mike Tyson-like haymakers to their face. Or they start to shiver and shake frantically because they fear your going to abuse them somehow. It's actually internally devastating to the owner too. All you can think of in your head is, "That poor little guy! What on god's green earth did your previous owner do to you". Then you start to consider a witch hunt to track down the previous owner and kick their ass 3 weeks from Sunday. See how they like it!

> Now transcend this with going on dates or even online dating. I can't tell you how many profiles I've lightly scanned and it's the same statements of pain sometimes verbatim but by different women and men. These people have really been put through the wringer and have been lied to, cheated on, used, abused, taken advantage of, and generally treated terribly time and time again. They're beyond jaded. Sad thing is, they want the whole world to know about it.

I'll give you an example.

Women -

- "Don't ask me for sexts I won't send them"
- "I'm sick of being used"
- "Is sex all you men think of"
- "Looking for a man who won't cheat"
- "Looking for a man who won't lie"
- "Looking for a kind gentleman"
- "No games, I just want to real deal"
- "Not looking for a hookup or DTF"
- "No I will not come to your house"
- "Please message me something more than, hey!"
- "I don't need your money or your nice car"
- "I can take care of myself"
- "I don't care that you have a 6 pack"
- "I'm proud of my curves"
- "I'm just looking to get to know people and see how it goes"
- "This is who I am, if you don't like it. TS"
- "I just want someone who won't ghost"

Men -

- "Don't play me for a fool"
- "I ain't your meal ticket"
- "You ain't getting a free date outta me"
- "I don't date thots (Hoes, sluts, skanks, bitches, and other derogatory phrases)
- "You can't turn a hoe into a housewife"
- "I have a job, a car and a nice house"
- "I got my own business"
- "I'll have my own business one day"
- "Used to own my own business"
- "Recently divorced"
- "Why are you women such bitches"
- "Can you ride?"
- "Just looking for a girl that won't break my heart"

- "I wish women would give me a chance"
- "I have 3 kids they're a package deal"
- "Don't people date the fat guy anymore?"
- "Enough with the snapchat filters"
- "Stop using group photos as your profile pic, girl "

Blargh blargh, blargh, blargh. Needy, needy, needy. Pain, pain and more pain. My life is so hard no one loves me and why won't someone treat me right. These people are crying out for help and they'll tell anyone who will hear them. But in reality, it only drives people further away. Or as the universe would have it, attracts the exact kind of people they want to avoid. Weird how that works. Some pricks out there really get off on stuff like that. If someone says, "Not DTF" that person who is DTF, will pursue them till they get what they want. It's kinda messed up, to be honest. But the world is littered with dating sociopaths.

These people harbor those emotions because of previous dating atrocities. They're not wrong and have every right to feel that way. But it's the way you do it, how much you let it affect your future, and if you're projecting that kind of emotion on your poor unsuspecting first date who has literally done nothing to you apart from showing up. Projecting previous relationship and dating mishaps on a potential mate is very unhealthy and you really have to find a way to acknowledge the pain and move on. The kind of person that you want, that high-quality individual. They have clairvoyance enough to know that you're projecting and they will not put up with it.

We've all been there at some point. We're very much like the shivering dog. These people go on dates but project that fear to the other person cause they're so worried it might happen again. I'm with you my friends, I truly am. I know the pain that it causes in your warm hearts when someone isn't who they say they are when someone swore to your face that they were different and that they would be with you through the hard times. Or worse, when someone isn't who you THINK they are. Those rose-tinted glasses were ripped off your face so violently and suddenly. Before you even had time to fully immerse yourself in the wildness of unbridled passion and the newness of pure affection. It was stripped from you. Or worse you were fully in with this person and they didn't even have a fraction of emotion towards your feelings, the whole time they were thinking left and you were thinking right. It's happened to all of us, no one is exempt from getting their heart shattered into a million pieces (A bit dramatic, but hey). That's okay. It's how we deal with those emotions and what we project publicly and to that individual, that's what matters.

Imagine this. You have an incredible first date and a 2nd and a 3rd, hell even a great 4th date. You actually feel like you've known this person forever. One uber-romantic evening, you are both in the mood and it happens. Glorious and magical sex, straight out of a Nicholas Sparks novel (Or Stephen King if that's what you're into). You wake up with a tremendous pep in your step. You text your closest friends and let them know of what beauties await with this newfound individual and now you're ready to take a chance on them and see where it goes. All you think about is how magical that night was. You fantasize about a wedding, meeting the parents walking dogs together, and buying your first house with them. You wait by your phone for days but nothing happens. Or you text the next day and get no response. After a few days, you call and text, and still nothing. That person is GONE. You cry, complain to your friends, or tell no one. Pretending it never happened. You delete them off all social media and swear that people are liars, bullshitters, and complete wastes of space.

1 - 3 months go by and you're ready again. This time you're different, guarded, unsure of yourself. Even if you like that person, you're afraid that it will surely happen again! So maybe you flake on the first date or the 3rd. Or you freak out when they go in for a kiss. This is the deep-rooted effect of "dating kicked dog syndrome". You may not know it yet, but it's ruining all of your

dating experiences until you acknowledge, try, and move on to improve them.

Sheesh. Could you imagine going into a store and trying to return an item? The cashier refuses to serve you. You're confused and you just want to return these jeans because they fit weird, you've even got the damn receipt. Eventually, the cashier confesses as to why they can't serve you. They explain that the last time a customer tried to return something they were rude, angry, and shouted at them. The cashier continues and explains that they don't want it to happen again.

How is that fair on you? You just want to return some jeans. Why should the previous actions of another customer affect you? How is that okay? It's one of the most dangerous things you can do to someone. Reacting with such high guarded emotional protection because of your previous pain. Do not force your previous emotional pain onto someone, your trust issues, or your intimacy concerns. It's just not fair to another person who has to deal with it. Trust me, eventually, they won't. No one wants to start things off as an emotional counselor. There will be a time you can open up about things of that nature. But you must always enter a dating scenario in good faith and drop your guard. Not a safety guard. But your emotional guard.

I know there's always going to be a counterargument. The right person will love you and put up with that no matter what, yada yada yada. That's true to some extent. But by that same token if the "right person" is truly grounded, smart, emotionally intelligent, and put together. They'll have clairvoyance enough to know they can be with someone who doesn't allow the "kick dog" syndrome to affect their dating lives, especially in the first few encounters. So they'll probably find someone with a stronger emotionally developed backbone. It works both ways. Which one are you more comfortable with? Before you jump into the next scenario of dating and possible relationships. You have to work on as many psychological kinks as you have.

What about this, you meet this person at an event and exchange numbers. They seem really cool and you're both yammering on about the latest Dua Lipa album and your love of music. It seems like a perfectly good conversation. You pull the trigger and guess what, she accepts and gives you her number. You set a date and you're both texting each other leading up to the date. The day comes and they show up. But something is different, the chemistry you both had that last Saturday is gone. The conversation is stale and opaque, small talk liters in and out and it just becomes boring as you glance outside the window every now and then to see what's out there. 45 minutes go by and that's it. You both call it time and leave on a very boring, cordial casual goodbye. Yikes. What happened you think to yourself? What changed? I did everything right last Saturday, the chemistry was there, I swear! Alas, all is lost and I will never make that much effort again look where it got me. We've all been there but you gotta keep trying.

Not all men and women are the same. What works with one will not always work with the other. You have to look at it this way just because you had a bad experience doesn't mean it's doomed to repeat itself, again and again, that's just the reality of it. Don't allow your past negative experiences to hurt your potential future with someone who is nothing like the previous lover in your life. People can see right through that and it's a really huge turn-off for some folks. Just be extremely careful with the morals you place on yourself that are a result of someone else's silly mistakes. The only dating morals you should ever make should be based on what you like. Not based on what negative experiences you've had. Look at the individual with a brand new pair of eyes and imagine all the good in them. It's okay to be extra vigilant and cognizant of them. But don't let that derail potential and immediate romantic inclinations that could very well come to pass.

30. Ask Good Questions!

So I've kinda touched on this a few times throughout this book but I want to go deeper and give you some great questions as well as explore why it's so very important to ask questions that leave long-lasting and romantic thoughts in their mind as you watch them drive away at the end of your date. You'll know deep down that you were able to build a deeper intellectual and sapiosexual connection. Asking questions also gives you a very rough compatibility scale. For example, if I ask a lady if she likes dogs and she says no. That's something to consider as a negative. Sounds kind of silly but that's a big deal to me. It's important to ask questions to really get to know someone but also find out if they're a good match.

Before I write anything else though I gotta give you a mental reminder. A reminder that you're not Sherlock Holmes. You are not trying to solve a case and question them to a point of exhaustion. Rather, you're asking these questions to foster a deeper and more meaningful interaction. That's where attraction builds, the more a person is allowed to talk and express how they feel the more attraction is growing and ultimately that's the idea of a first date. Starting with a light jog, a quick sprint then a nice long marathon! The conversation is a turn-taking exercise unless you're a psychologist with a patient. It's not meant to be one-sided. It's a slippery road too, most people end up being the questioners. Sometimes it's just their nature. But you have to be careful where it's not just them asking you all the questions even if they do like it. You want to give them enough air time too, if not more.

I once went out with a very sophisticated woman. She asked intriguing and thought-provoking questions. I loved every minute of it. But halfway through the date, I realized we were just talking about me. So I put a stop to it and started asking her questions. Thank goodness I did too. Or she would have indeed ended up being a 1-hour shrink.

Questions are important because it allows you to realize and open up small windows of vulnerability which in turn evoke power punches of emotion. Once you ask a question that lights them up and they are far more eager to interact, build on that and then follow suit with the other questions I'm going to give you. The more you are allowed to be free and talk about the things you truly love, things you desire, and things that you aspire towards. The more you're able to open up and feel some kind of natural attraction.

Don't worry about small essences of silence. That doesn't mean it won't work with the two of you. Just means you're literally meeting for the first time. Always take that into consideration. People are rarely chatty Kathy's immediately. Like everything else it takes time. True long-lasting relationships with that special someone will always come down to a matter of time and patience. So don't rush anything.

It's actually kind of funny to me that dating apps have made it so you can find someone you think is very attractive by the comfort of sitting on a toilet seat. But it doesn't change a simple thing that a lot of people struggle with.

That's honest, indivisible, and scintillating conversation. We are so connected to things that are all technology-based these days. Your phones, laptops, cars, televisions, and all that other good stuff. Because of this, some people are conversationally stunted. The bar for basic informative conversation is completely on the floor, so these next few paragraphs will make things far easier for you. This is why it's up to you to be more connected to personal conversations than ever. Our society knows we're over-connected and a lot of people in the single/dating world are craving a change. So start to work on your questioning capabilities. We all know some of the major causes right? Social media, texting, online dating, and Instagram culture have tossed the backseat to genuine and authentic conversations people don't really know how to speak on a first date. There is an abundance of options out there right now for everyone. So why not make a focused effort for one person? That's a mentality that a lot of people are struggling with right now.

I like the idea of having at least 10 - 15 pre-date questions because it means that witty banter and great moments can be created inside those questions. I mean who doesn't like talking about what they'd do if they won the lottery or their favorite taco stand or the best movie they have ever watched. I get it, you're confident and maybe you don't need questions. But there's a difference between dating competency and dating confidence. When you're competent in dating it means you have very high social EQ and actually take the time to get better and understand you're not the best human ever. When you're confident in dating it means you show up to date with no plan at all with little concern for the person you're with. Avoid that. It's human nature to like having a conversation and nature gets far more human when you ask questions that appeal, stick, and build an alluring resonance with that gorgeous individual. Don't worry it's not an unnatural thing to have some pre-prescribed questions. By the grace of you going out of your way to plan and meet someone for a date is all intentional so there are not too many things "natural" about it. You just have to figure out a way to slide the questions in and allow them to grow another organic branch to build on. The questions are a playing field but remember, you make the plays. If you're with a pretty exceptional date you'll bounce off each other pretty well.

You've bought this book because you're in the top 5 percentile of people who want to be better and who realize the best way to stand out in the herd of dating potentials is to be different, educated, and most importantly master the art of conversation and questioning. Most detectives get their guys and throw them in jail because they were effective questionnaires. Now I'm not asking you guys to go full Jessica Jones. But I'm trying to help you realize that questioning is one of the most effective tools you can use to really design a masterpiece of conversation.

Small talk isn't the worst thing out there and if the whole date happens to be about nothing but small talks so be it. But you, you're different. You can do better than small talk.

So let's crack on to the good stuff, shall we? What are some of the most thought-provoking questions!? I've gone through over 100 different articles and 7 books, I had to dig between satirical posts, serious posts, and angry posts just to give you guys the best. Yes, 3 months of mind-numbing articles, posts, and stories. There were some exceptional ones though. So no more lollygagging here's my best questions:

1. Are you working on anything awesome outside of work?

2. What's the best gift you've ever received/given?

3. How do you usually spend most of your time?

4. What are some of your best vacation stories?

5. So what crazy things happened today?

6. What was the best and worst part of your day today?

7. Do you have any cool pieces of advice someone has given to you that really stuck around?

8. What kind of friends do you typically hang with?

9. Shitty kid? Or a good kid growing up?

10. Best TV show of all time?

11. If you could have dinner with anyone dead or alive who would it be and why?

12. Have you considered how you'll die?

13. What's a healthy relationship to you?

14. Does my butt look big in these pants?

15. What's the best part of your job?

16. What are some random facts about you?

17. Do you know of anyone who might think you two are dating or in a relationship right now?

18. What's Your Favorite Place on Earth?

19. Who Are the Special People in Your Life?

20. What's Something You're Proud of?

21. What celebrities annoy you?

22. Any good music you're listening to these days?

23. Are You a Morning Person or a Night Owl?

24. What Would Constitute a "Perfect" Day For You?

25. What's the Last TV Show You Binged or Re-Watched?

26. How did you and your best-friend meet, and how did they become your best friend?

27. If I could talk to your friends, what is the most embarrassing story about you that they would tell me?

28. What do you have to apologize for most often?

29. What's the Best Gift You've Ever Been Given?

Be individual. Always go for questions that spawn figments of emotion.

31. Who Asks Who Out?

Indeed.

In this progressive era, we live in, who asks who out? Have roles really changed that much? Are we finally experiencing some major shift in dating?

Short answer, no.

If you didn't already know in this book so far. Dating hasn't evolved too much in the gender roles department for the most part. Yes, there have been smatterings of small impactful changes across the last few decades. Women no longer have to "accidentally" drop their handkerchief to show a man interest. But not enough has really changed. I would imagine if that happened in current times the man would be walking by on his phone and walk on it with his dirty ass Vans.

Asking someone out is a gender role that hasn't much shifted either. Like I said in the "Who Pays?" chapter, so many other things in society have been progressively changing for good but who asks who out has progressed at around 3 miles per hour on a 70mph freeway. The men still shoulder most of the responsibility of doing this. Asking someone out isn't a benign and excruciating process but it does make it a little harder to gauge interest level, even if they say yes to going out with you. They could want a free meal, just something to do, get out of the house, find a friend, and so forth. I think for the most part they are interested, but there still could be those other thoughts in play. I mean they still have dances for high schoolers once a year where the women ask the men. And people make such a big deal about it because typically women don't ask men to dances or proms. Some do, for sure. But most don't. It's like dating is still stuck in the '50s.

It's hard for both men and women. Even though men have a bit more social pressure to do the asking. Women also suffer a paradoxical issue of interest too. Let's break it down. I'll do it this way. First for the men and then flip it around so you can see how women deal with it on their end after having to be the recipient of the asking out and vice versa. Don't get me wrong I'm a bloke and I don't assume to speak on behalf of women and generalize them. But based on the focus groups I've had and conversations I've had with the opposite sex, this is where most of my information comes from.

Men and Asking Out:

So what's it like? So here are some obvious things you might already know. The men typically ask the women out and pursue until they feel like they have a good understanding of who the person is, how interested they are if they're interested at all, and so on. Here's what you might not know.

Because it's expected and is the norm for them to do the asking. It means that when it comes to dating. Statistically, men will face far more rejection than women and have to go through the harder task of really knowing if the women are interested. I mean think about it. If you ask a woman out because you kinda like her. It's literally a shot in the dark. There's no real guaranteed way you'll know 100% with surety that she's interested before you shoot your shot, yes you could receive a smile a glance, and some clear signals of interest but even then depending on the conversation it can all go sour. Then even if you find a woman who's interested dependent on her specifications of what she typically finds attractive, the longer you get to know her. Who knows how long the attraction on her part will last. Because YOU initiated the first date and possibly the second and third. In the back of your mind no matter how confident you are they'll still be a small shred of doubt. The only real way you'll know she's interested is if she vocalizes how she feels or you've been together for a few weeks.

Now I'm not saying this to paint the men as victims or to deter you if you are a man. But I'm letting you know there's no way around rejection and no matter who you are you're going to experience a lot of it. You can't play football without getting sacked. You can't shoot hoops without missing. That's just the way it goes. A lot of women out there, even modern progressive women still very much like the idea of being pursued, they want to embrace their femininity and feel wanted. So for the most part like it all lump you have to come face to face with the art of rejection and understand as a man you'll have to do the initial groundwork for a short while.

Scenario A:

Check this out. You've been talking to this lovely lady for about 20 minutes at this house warming party of a friend. She seems very interested, she's been laughing at your jokes, maintaining eye contact and you two both have a lot in common. You feel like the attraction is mutual so you pull the trigger and you ask her out:

You: You know what.

Her: What?

You: We should go to that art gallery we were talking about

Her: Oh I'm sorry I have a boyfriend

You: Ah, no worries.

Bahhh.

Awkward.

But this will make you stronger. Embrace it like a warm hug from your granny.

Do you see where I'm coming from though? There's no way you could have known. It's not her fault either. She was just being polite and having a friendly conversation with a nice guy at a party. That's just it though. You never really know. But if you feel like it's worth a shot you have gotta take it, your biggest regret will always be what could have been and not what's already come to pass. So long as you take the rejection like a gentleman and try and make the girl not feel weird afterward you should be fine. But check this scenario out.

Scenario B:

So you've been talking to this great woman for about 20 minutes at this work conference in your city. She works for another company and you're both project managers. Your both laughing giddily at the silly imbeciles who just don't understand your craft. You're getting along so well and there's a strong connection. The exact same signs are there like when you spoke to that girl at the house party. But you don't want to get rejected again. You want to be respectful with it being a work conference and all. Keep it professional and all that. Yes, yes.

Her: So what part of the Bay area do you live in?

Him: San Jose, actually.

Her: Cool, I live in San Mateo.

Him: Oh nice, so we're kinda neighbors!

Her: Exactly!

Him: Okay cool, well hopefully I'll see you around?

Her: Yeah, I really hope so. Sooner rather than later.

She was super interested. The girl walks away wondering why the guy didn't ask for her number. She gave him all the signs. Laughed at his jokes. Even agreed that they're kinda neighbors. She's confused and wonders why he wasn't interested.

Ya, see! This shit doesn't work. Having the social emphasis placed on the man to do the asking doesn't always work. It's a broken and flawed expectation especially now. This lady was very much interested. Because she subconsciously has bought into these societal normalities she stuck around waiting for him to ask her and he didn't. He was such a "kicked dog" he didn't want to face another rejection. Especially at a work business conference. She thought she was making it very clear.

Imagine how many women have missed out on great guys with who they could have been compatible because they didn't want to make the first move of asking them out. Or expected the man to "read the signs". Of course, the argument could be made by women, "Well the kind of man I'm looking for needs to have to balls to ask me out". This could be true. But is that the man you're compatible with? Look if you want something, go out there and get it! I'm giving you vocal permission. Man or woman, take a chance. Gender roles be damned. Like I've mentioned an abundance of times. This book is for you to do things differently than you've ever done them before. Forsake any kind of expectations, release that ego and go with a positive and confident mindset.

I've heard the counterargument from women and it's valid to some degree. When I spoke to my focus group about who asks who out. A lot of them said. If a woman is too forward with asking a man out she's seen as a slut or easy, or perhaps maybe way too eager. Some of them mentioned it even emasculates a man. What!?

Look if some of you guys out there feel emasculated when a woman asks you out. Buck up your ideas and stop being such an insecure chump. Embrace a confident woman with open arms. Some of the women said they don't want to make it easy for the guy. Haha, what!? Make it easy? How about making it equal. Or make it honest with how you feel. We have to stop playing these games people.

Sometimes I feel like I'm in the freaking twilight zone. We talk about all these wonderful things about female empowerment and I'm all in. Trust me I'm for it.

- Women are strong
- Women are confident
- Women are empowered
- Equal pay
- Equal rights
- Anything a man can do women can too
- Women are strong mothers
- Women are full of wisdom
- Women should be equal to men.

All of these things are true. And then some. So why is it that when it comes to dating and being a little forward with what you want in terms of relationship/dating pursuit? A lot of women leave some of that if not all of the emphasis on the man.

If you're reading or listening to this banging on the car stereo or screenshotting this piece of the book to Bustle.com. Pump your breaks. This is not a bash on women. I'm merely suggesting that we try as a human race to change it up a bit. I'm suggesting that now more than ever women can be pursuers too, and get what they want. People who still want to live in the past and label as much as they can kiss your ass. Who cares what they think. Chances are you'll never see them again.

Imagine sitting at a restaurant as a woman. The waiter comes along and asks for your order. You talk about what kind of sauces you like on the meal, how spicy you like it, the meats or veggies you like, and how hot you like your food. The waiter appreciates your detail then asks:

Waiter: This is all great information, thank you so much. What would you like to eat from our menu?

Her: What!? I gave you all the signs you should just know

Waiter: I'm sorry ma'am I'm confused.

Her: How can you be confused, I gave you all the signals. You need to step up and be a man.

Waiter: I'm sorry ma'am but I'm going to have to ask you to leave.

Sounds crazy right. But this is how it can be when you don't go for what you want. If one of my guy friends tells me he met a really awesome girl at the grocery store and engaged in amazing conversation. I'd say why didn't you ask her out. If he says, "I sent her all the signs dude, she didn't do anything". We'd all be like.

"What the hell!? You could have at least gotten her number". Right?

So why is that same logic not applied to women if they're interested?

Ya see.

It just doesn't work.

I looked online at around 67 articles. My search criteria was "Who asks who out on the first date".

And...

HOLY SHIT!

There were titles like this.

- 4 Ways to get a guy to ask you out
- How to send signals so HE knows what to do
- This tip will get a guy to ask you out
- Should I ask him out? How to be more daring in dating

- Why don't guys ask me out?
- Why girls shouldn't ask guys out on dates
- Who should come up with the first date idea
- Does asking a girl out mean your boyfriend and girlfriend (Clearly written by a 12-year-old)
- Why do guys wait so long to ask for my number?
- How should a Christian guy ask a girl out?
- Should women ask men out on first dates?
- 14 men tell us why they want women to initiate a date
- Is it okay to use LinkedIn to ask someone on a date
- Is it sexual harassment to ask someone for a date at work?
- What do I do when he hasn't asked me out?

Ya, see!

You get the gist here. There are literally thousands of articles only reinforcing women that asking someone out for a date is all on the man. He should KNOW. Ladies, the notion of playing hard to get is incredibly dated. To be honest, if there are men that get off on that, they'd probably not be the ones for you.

I read one article that was some of the worst dating advice I had ever read. "Reasons I Tell Guys I Can't Hang Out Last-Minute (Even When I Can).

SMDH.

Really!? The title alone is INCREDIBLY disingenuous. You're already starting your dating escapades off with a lie. What in the "How to Lose a Guy in 10 Days" bullshit is this. The article was cringe-worthy. She continues with these 4 subheadings. "He'll learn he needs to plan ahead if he wants to see you". "You'll set the pace in the relationship". These just reek of narcissism and are not healthy. This is sending dating backward and is encouraging manipulative behavior from the start.

There's social pressure too. Guys who can't muster up the courage to speak to a woman in a bar or club may be looked down on by their male peers, as society has deemed it be more masculine that you be a "real man" and go speak to her.

Two weeks later I met with 8 guys and this is what they have to say.

Tony 31: "Yeah it's pretty cool when a girl asks you to go on a date.

I mean she's a woman so all she'd have to do is breath the word date and I'd say yes, or she has to be cute"

Cotton 22: "It's kinda random, to be honest, but I dig it"

Jim 26: 'I'm happy when a chick doesn't expect me to organize all the time. I'm happy to plan dates but if they like me too, every now and then they should do something"

Troy 33: "I'm a man, can't be having no female ask me out. A grown-ass man takes care of his lady and does the chasing. It's that simple, bruh"

Whitaker 25: "When a woman takes control every now and then it's very sexy".

Liam 29: "So I've been doing the online thing for a few months now. What's funny to me is most girls I match with. Unless I send the first message they won't. Which is a kinda weird. They obviously think I'm hot otherwise they wouldn't have swiped right too. So when I speak to a girl on Tinder or somethin and she asks me out. I'm very interested and I know she might smash"

Stephen 23: "So long as there's no pressure. I'm not trying to marry her if she asks me out. I hope she wouldn't feel like anything could happen"

(Yeah good one Stephen)

DeShaun 26: "I feel like if she's asks me then I already know she's interested. Girls don't ask unless they really like the guy and that sounds good to me".

Not the most definitive by any means but I think you get the idea. People are starting to wise up. The old guards respecting the paradigm of the man asking the women first are still there yes. But more and more men are harboring an expectation that women will step up to the plate and take the risk of asking the guy out too. If we truly want to have relationship equality it has to start now.

Women and asking out:

Well, let's start with the obvious notion of a man asking the woman out and how she might feel. I compiled conversations and focus groups around 6 weeks for this one.

In one sentence. It comes down to two factors.

Is she attracted to you, or not.

Yes I know, it sounds very absolute but that's my one-sentence summary.

I'll never forget this, it was the last week of my focus group discussing "Who asks who out". Afterward, we decided to get some drinks. These women were, very attractive, highly intelligent, and confident. Being around them was great for insights. But as we were there they were all approached as a group about 4 times. Often the man or men approaching them would ask what I was doing there. Yeah, I get it, I guess it did look kinda weird. They probably thought I was the pimp.

Some of these men had good openers I'll say. Polite, friendly, and jovial gentlemen. Yet some of the women labeled them, creepy, try-hard, and wouldn't take the hint. The last group of guys came over and said pretty much the exact same shit as the 3 guys prior to that. You know, "where you from", "what do you do for work?" "How do you all know each other". Stuff like that. Verbatim what the other guys said 30 minutes beforehand. The women were enamored on this occasion.

The difference, these guys were significantly attractive and had far better delivery and body language. They were confident and before they even said anything, it showed. You see when some women are attracted to a man, it doesn't really matter what he says so long as he isn't a dick. But these are the only things applicable in cold interactions. What's a cold interaction? Meeting someone you don't know.

The gym, elevator, supermarket, bar, club, event, and so forth. These are places where some women routinely receive cold interactions by would-be suitors who find them attractive. A pretty attractive woman gets hit on whether subtly or directly at least every other day. That's a lot of days in the year. Unless she's a shut-in or something. Even then if she's only out of the house once a week that's 26 times a year if we go by the every other day principle that's 182.5 days a year! It's insane. Now seen as we're in the midst of a pandemic Let's slash that in half that's still 91 days a year. That doesn't even include the random social media advances she may get.

So with all that said now you have a better understanding of why most women make a minimal effort when it comes to asking a man out on a date unless they really, really like him. Cause in most cases they don't really have to. So it happens, trust me it does, but as I said, it's usually extenuating circumstances.

But there are other reasons too. These reasons are actually kinda funny but a little sad too. I decided to bust out the old Twitter account and look up what women were saying when they took the initiative and asked guys out. Be warned these reactions are not for the faint of heart. If your mums in the car or a family member are next to you as you read this. Make sure you're in a private.

Here are some reactions:

Tweet A: You want to go on a date?

Response: Would love to

Tweet B: Would you maybe wanna see **Just Cause** with me this Friday

Response: Absolutely

Tweet C: Wanna go on a date this Tuesday

Response: Heyyyyyy, yeah that sounds dope. So you're taking me out?

Then there was this :

Tweet D: Erm this is kinda awkward but do you wanna go on a date with me?

Response: It won't go anywhere so no point.

At least that guy was honest. But in her tweet for this screenshot, she said "Never again". Imagine if men had that mentality. No women would get asked out.

But this is exactly my point, there's such a huge imbalance but the mere thought of a woman being bold enough to ask out a guy is a big deal.

One lady tweeted with a bold attestation, "I did it!" As if to say it was such a big step. But here's the thing. To her it was! To a lot of women, it is.

I wonder how many women would get what they truly desired if they just asked for it, especially when it comes to dating. Men don't mind shouldering the work for the most part. But try it on for size it might work. If you've both matched on a dating app he clearly likes you. So definitely ask! But only if you actually want to meet them. Obviously, if he turns out to be a dirty little creeper, unmatch. Or if you meet him in a grocery store and he's looking at your chest as if it's corn on the cob. Abandon ship and pretend you have a phone call.

Trust me the truth is out there. In a match.com survey over 5509 men women took. It attested that 95% of men were in favor of women asking for their number. 95%!! Holy shit. Still, scared to ask? Don't be the odds are clearly in your favor.

When you as a woman wait for men to ask you, you rarely get to choose. Instead, you get someone asking you out where it could go either way, it's not the worst thing in the world. But when you ask the man out, it's who you like and who you actually want to get to know, it's such a better feeling and it embodies true feminine power. But don't take my word for it, I'm a bloke. An article was written by Starre Vartan. **S**he mentions some pretty cool details. She goes on to say, that "Men Like it" and that most men would rarely say no because it happens so little. She continues and laments that it's unfair to put all the emphasis on the man to ask and some men get a lot of anxiety. She mentions the notion of harassment. When men are presumed to have most of the power when it comes to asking they may very well not take no for a clear-cut answer and think the woman is playing hard to get. I'm sure we've all heard stories of some poor woman who has given a number away or worse had sex with someone just cause this guy was so fucking persistent. Take the power back and start doing some asking. The only real thing that can happen from this is growth, empowerment and a different perspective you might not otherwise have had.

To all you people reading this thinking, a real man asks the woman out! I challenge you to ask out 10 guys in a month then let me know how you feel about it. If an NBA player, astronaut, lawyer, doctor, race car driver, fast food worker, electrician all say, "Try walking a mile in my shoes". That's not something you can pick up one day. However, if you're a woman attempting to ask out 10 different guys in a month. You can very well start tomorrow. If you haven't even got the fortitude to do that. Imagine how it is for the average dude who has to ask out 50 women a year just to get 5 - 10 dates. Out of those 10 dates, none of them may even pan out.

See, it's kinda hard out there for a bloke. Men are not impervious from rejection, sure we might be able to handle it a bit better as we'll often be shooting our shot. But it hurts just the same when you put yourself out there and get shut down. Some shutdowns are worse than others.

Yes, I know this is a section for the ladies. But as you can see when it comes to asking out there isn't much emphasis on them being the primary facilitators. The men out there that can flirt, tease, permeate masculinity and speak to women effortlessly are heroes in real life and even bigger heroes in most media. But then look at it on the flip side. Women who are incredibly intelligent, can flirt easily, and ask men out at a whim are almost slut shamed and called ho's, easy and giving it away. Sometimes by their female counterparts. So women from birth are passively programmed to be pursued. So I totally understand if that's not even close to the realm of reality for any given woman to do the asking.

Conclusion:

There is no conclusion.

Why? Because you have just started. Because you are on a brand new journey of positive self-discovery.

Because you realize that you are unique. That you are a prize to someone and quite frankly to a lot of people.

Now you have so many more tools and small facets of understanding to go out there and really start making a huge impact in your romantic future.

I know you've been hurt, I know sometimes you get lonely. I know it hasn't been easy.
But never ever under any circumstances should you give up on finding someone.

Never give up.

Cause in most cases you're so much closer than you think and you owe it to yourself to try new things and start approaching things with a different paradigm altogether.

Look inward and realize that there are some things you have to change for yourself if you want to see different results.

Things will never just come to you. You must go out there and get them! Let the world know how wonderful you are.

Let them know that you are worthy of love. That you are a gorgeous individual. Because you are.

I believe you bought this book because you want to change. You want things to change. If you've made it this far I promise you you will see change.

Why?

It doesn't matter what you're doing so long as you're doing something.,

The mere fact that you got this book means you're willing to go that extra step that quite frankly. Most people are not willing to do.

I'm rooting for you. I believe in you and I know you believe in yourself.

You might make mistakes, but you can recover and keep going. Please never lose hope over a minor setback. Please don't let people take that power from you. It's yours and you can master how you feel about any given situation.

Don't allow your past to be reflective of how your future may be.

Please be open to giving and receiving love, believe that you will attract loving, supportive, committed partners who are consistent and never give up on who you truly are and the greatness you can become!

Always and I mean always be grateful for the love you receive from friends, family, strangers, and of course that person we're all waiting for you to meet.

Deep down in your heart please let go and forgive others for past relationship transgressions. They have to deal with that now. Not you.

Always enter every interaction in good faith.

If you sincerely enjoyed this book and there was at least one chapter that helped. Give me a review. I'd love to hear what stuck and continue spreading that message together.

Dating is a bit of a mess at the moment.

Let's change it one step at a time. Let's be the change we want to see.

Love,

Trey Richard Hamilton

Made in United States
Troutdale, OR
08/01/2023

11729816R00148